I have a love-hate relat of Larry
Hurtado's massive sc Christian
understandings of J it to get
Honoring the Son into it puts in
front of them all of his best thinking; on the other hand, I have been
reading Hurtado's works for 30 years, book by book, article by article. Need I say it took lots of work to read his body of work? Need
I say now that we have all his major thoughts now available in one
evening's reading? One generation's efforts are the next generation's
beginning points, so start here. You'll rise up and call me blessed!

—**Scot McKnight**, Julius R. Mantey Professor of
New Testament, Northern Seminary

When I was taking a course on the history of New Testament interpretation in 1990, we read Wilhelm Bousset's book on the emergence of the worship of Jesus as Deity as *the* landmark work. In the
same course today, we would be reading Bousset alongside Larry
Hurtado, often in point-counterpoint fashion. Hurtado's work on
this key issue—how Jesus came to be recognized as divine—is of
central importance not only to students of early Christianity but
indeed to all who *worship* Jesus, and it is with great excitement that
I hold in my hand so accessible a summary of his decades of sift-
ing through the evidence, a book I can recommend not only to my
seminary students but to everyone in my congregation who ever
asks the question.

—**David A. deSilva**, Trustees' Distinguished Professor of New
Testament and Greek, Ashland Theological Seminary

It is thirty years since Larry Hurtado's first book on early Christian
devotion to Jesus burst upon the scene—and changed everything
scholars previously assumed about the development of Christology
and even Christianity itself. Over the last three decades, Hurtado

has followed that up with ever larger and more detailed volumes, demonstrating the evidence for his view that the first Christians, despite their Jewish identity, worshipped Jesus alongside God the Father. In this little book, Hurtado sets out the steps of his main argument clearly and logically with admirable precision and conciseness, undergirded by years of scholarship and setting it within current academic debate. This book is a godsend (literally!) to the thinking believer and the inquiring searcher alike—and is greatly to be welcomed and applauded.

—**The Revd Canon Prof Richard Burridge FKC**, dean and professor of biblical interpretation, King's College, London

Honoring the Son is a wonderfully clear distillation of decades of research and writing done by Larry Hurtado on the issue that he, more than any biblical scholar, has brought to prominence in the study of early Christology: devotional practice offered to Jesus along with God by monotheistic Jews within the first two decades of Christianity. Those readers who are unfamiliar with Hurtado will find here an introduction to this important subject that is accessible and succinct. This slim volume is packed with observations and conclusions that are both historically sound and theologically profound.

—**Charles A. Gieschen**, professor of exegetical theology, Concordia Theological Seminary

Larry Hurtado stands out as one of the most influential scholars in the study of earliest Christianity. *Honoring the Son* captures his basic insights, revealing the motors that drove early Jesus-devotion as it drew on Jewish theological resources and infiltrated the Roman world. Easy to read but full of substance, this little book is "the pocket Hurtado" that will benefit readers of all kinds.

—**Bruce Longenecker**, Melton Chair of Religion, Baylor University

HONORING THE SON

HONORING THE SON

JESUS IN EARLIEST CHRISTIAN DEVOTIONAL PRACTICE

Larry W. Hurtado

SNAPSHOTS

MICHAEL F. BIRD, SERIES EDITOR

LEXHAM PRESS

Honoring the Son: Jesus in Earliest Christian Devotional Practice
Snapshots, edited by Michael F. Bird

Copyright © 2018 Larry W. Hurtado

Lexham Press, 1313 Commercial St., Bellingham, WA 98225
LexhamPress.com

Print ISBN 9781683590965
Digital ISBN 9781683590972

Series Editor: Michael F. Bird
Lexham Editorial Team: Eric Bosell, Derek Brown, and Jeff Reimer
Cover Design: Brittany Schrock
Typesetting: Kathy Curtis

CONTENTS

When Professor Doctor Martin Hengel wrote his endorsement of Larry Hurtado's book *One God One Lord* (1988),[1] he made a rather prophetic statement. He wrote in the publisher's blurb:

> This very informative, interesting, and revolutionary book gathers in a masterly manner the results of scholarly experts in many countries who are in some way forming a new "Religionsgeschichtliche Schule." I know of few recent books which promote our understanding of early Christology so much as this volume.

Now Hengel himself played a pivotal role in establishing this new history of religions school (*religionsgeschichtliche Schule*). For he argued persuasively in various publications that Judaism had been Hellenized for centuries before the birth of Jesus and that the Judaisms of late antiquity, not pagan religions, provided

---

1. Larry W. Hurtado, *One God, One Lord: Early Christian Devotion and Ancient Jewish Monotheism* (Philadelphia: Fortress Press, 1988).

the rich soils into which the movement founded by and on Jesus had been planted and thrived.

Hengel's words were prophetic first because he was speaking the truth; a sea change was taking place in New Testament studies. Prior to Hengel, scholars typically began with the assumption that pagan influences flooded into the "church" and became the key shaping factors in the community's Christology. The latter school, however, in the decades following the Holocaust, took a different, more generous view toward the Judaisms of late antiquity. Rather than seeing Second Temple Judaism as a religion in deep decline, Hurtado and many other scholars regard it as the well that fed and nourished the worship and spiritual life of the community of Jesus.

But Hengel's words were prophetic also because he said them about the book of a scholar who was on track to become the dean of the new *Schule* (school). In fact, one could say that Hurtado's work, more than the work any other scholar, has helped form a consensus around the forces and factors that led to the early Christian devotion to Jesus in Jewish-gentile circles.

If Wilhelm Bousset had been the leading light of the Germany-based history of religions school in the early decades of the twentieth century, Larry Hurtado has become the leading figure of a new generation of scholars. He has published dozens of articles and a number of important books that address some of the most pivotal questions about Christian origins: How and when did the followers of Jesus begin to worship him and regard him as divine? How did Jewish monotheism contribute to or detract from how early Christians came to think of Jesus? What role did religious experience play in creating this new movement? In addition, at the University of Manitoba and University of Edinburgh Hurtado mentored a generation of students and scholars who have contributed in one way or another to posing and answering these questions. Few scholars have one Festschrift written in their honor. Hurtado has two: one by colleagues (both those who agree with him and those who do not)[2] and the other by his students.[3]

Hurtado is a founding member of the early high Christology club, an informal fellowship of scholars from various continents, backgrounds, and institutional affiliations. All "members" make the case, in one way or another, that a divine Christology emerges early among Jewish Christians; it is not the result of decades or centuries of assimilation with Greek and Roman ideas. Hurtado has been a pioneer in those discussions through his research and mentoring of students as well as colleagues. The significance of his research has been underscored recently by the collection and publication of all his articles on the topic of Christ-devotion as an anchor book in a new series called Library of Early Christology.[4]

In this book you have the core of Larry Hurtado's contribution to key aspects, perhaps the most important aspects, of Christian origins. Behind each paragraph is an article or a monograph either Hurtado himself or another scholar has written. Hurtado makes his case in dialogue with many supporters and detractors. If you dig down into the footnotes, you will find evidence of this dialogue, along with a wealth of information drawn from both primary and secondary sources. If we can

---

2. David B. Capes et al., eds., *Israel's God and Rebecca's Children: Christology and Community in Early Judaism and Christianity* (Waco, TX: Baylor University Press, 2008). In fact, this Festschrift honored Larry Hurtado and Alan F. Segal, a Jewish scholar who was also a founding member of the early high Christology club.

3. Chris Keith and Dieter T. Roth, eds., *Mark, Manuscripts, and Monotheism: Essays in Honor of Larry W. Hurtado*, Library of New Testament Studies (Edinburgh: T&T Clark/Bloomsbury, 2014).

4. Larry W. Hurtado, *Ancient Jewish Monotheism and Early Christian Jesus-Devotion: The Context and Character of Christological Faith*, Library of Early Christology (Waco, TX: Baylor University Press, 2017).

say anything about Hurtado's work, it is this: his work is well researched, clearly argued, and generous to those with whom he disagrees. Even as he finds fault with some of the arguments and conclusions by Maurice Casey, J. D. G. Dunn, Adela Yarbro Collins, and Bart Ehrman, he also finds value in their methods and approaches.

Beyond this, Hurtado has done a great deal to help us understand the true context of Roman-era religions, including Judaism and Christianity. While most today think of "religion" primarily as a system of beliefs, Hurtado makes a cogent case from the evidence that in the Roman era "religion" was more a matter of practice than beliefs; and there is no practice more central to Roman religions than worship.

Christians (and Jews for that matter) became infamous among their Roman neighbors not for what they did but for what they would not do; they would not worship the many deities that undergirded Roman society. As a result early Christ followers were called "atheists" and declared a clear and present danger to the empire.

In the end, for Hurtado, early Christianity was distinct from other religions by a constellation of devotional practices that featured Jesus as the rightful recipient. It was distinct from Judaism because it included the risen Jesus as a recipient of worship along with God. It was distinct from other Roman-era religions because it excluded the worship of all gods except the one, true God of Israel and the man seated at his right hand. If we wish to understand how Christianity began, Hurtado insists that we focus on worship, not beliefs or doctrines. But this novel perspective on the one God of Israel was not ditheism (the recognition and worship of two, distinct gods); it was a "mutation" of Jewish devotional practices. For decades Hurtado has described the early Christian practices as a "mutation" of its parent traditions, but it is here, in this book, that he offers the clearest description of what he meant:

> By the term "mutation" I mean a development that has both recognizable connections with the "parent" religious tradition (in this case, ancient Judaism) and also identifiably new features that distinguish the development from its parent tradition. I have also characterized the early Christian development as comprising a "dyadic" devotional pattern in which the risen/exalted Jesus featured centrally and uniquely with God as virtually a co-recipient of cultic devotion (pp. 42–43).

In many of his earlier writings Professor Hurtado describes the devotional pattern of early Christianity as "binitarian"; but in more recent publications he has abandoned that term because of the historical baggage it bears due to the later trinitarian controversies. For Hurtado, the term "dyadic" strikes the right tone to describe what is at the heart of early Christian worship.

Put simply, the first followers of Jesus were convinced that God required them to reverence Jesus. Those convictions were based on several factors: (1) how they remembered Jesus; (2) God's raising of Jesus and exalting him to his right hand; (3) post-Easter prophecies and religious experience; and (4) a phenomenon known as "charismatic exegesis." Though it seems to Hurtado a secondary factor, how believers read and reread their Scriptures (roughly equivalent to our "Old Testament") in light of the life, death, burial, and resurrection of Jesus proved to be an important factor in what Christianity becomes. In charismatic exegesis Old Testament stories are replotted on a new-covenant and new-creation grid so that Jesus takes on a remarkable role in Israel's story and is bestowed with the divine name and status. Hurtado, more than any scholar I know, has helped us grapple with these novel and remarkable features of early Christianity.

David B. Capes
Wheaton College

ACKNOWLEDGMENTS

My thanks to Michael Bird for suggesting that I develop this little book and to Derek Brown (one of my former PhD students) for shepherding it through the publication process. The origins of this book lie in a paper presented in a symposium held at New Orleans Baptist Theological Seminary in February 2016. For this publication, I have expanded the discussion considerably, particularly in giving a much fuller account of the scholarly context for my own work.

As will be apparent from the footnotes and bibliography, the study of devotion to Jesus (or early "Christology," as it is often called) has become a major focus of scholarly effort over the last several decades. I have learned a lot from the work of other scholars, even if I found myself disagreeing at times. The intense interest in the origins of the remarkable devotion to Jesus that appeared so early and so quickly after his crucifixion justifiably continues to draw scholarly attention, including the production of PhD theses by younger scholars. I hope that my efforts have been of some benefit—or at least have stimulated others to address the relevant questions.

My own focus is historical in an effort to understand, in the terms and intellectual categories of those who produced that ancient evidence, what the earliest evidence about Jesus-devotion tells us. This is sometimes frustrating to those who want to pose questions in term that developed later in Christian thought, the "ontological" categories that became so prominent in the classical creeds. My focus on the earlier terms and actions with which Christians expressed their devotion to Jesus does not connote a rejection of those later theological developments. I simply think that it is important to read texts in the terms and categories that were contemporary with them, whatever theological reflection we may subsequently take up.

As in a number of prior publications, my emphasis here is on the devotional actions that were expressive of earliest Jesus-devotion. I remain convinced that the most significant development in the history of earliest Christianity was the inclusion of the exalted Jesus as a recipient of worship. The following pages offer a condensed rationale for that view.

CHAPTER 1

INTRODUCTION

In the following pages, I want to make these points: (1) In the ancient Roman world, worship was the key expression of "religion," not beliefs and confessional formulas; (2) the key distinguishing feature that marked off Roman-era Judaism in the larger religious environment was its cultic exclusivity, the refusal to worship any deity other than the God of Israel; (3) this exclusivity involved refusal also to worship the adjutants of the biblical God, not simply foreign deities; (4) in this context, the emergent place of Jesus in earliest Christian worship and devotional practice along with God in a "dyadic" devotional pattern represents something highly notable, even more significant historically than the familiar christological titles and confessional formulas; and (5) the place of Jesus in early Christian devotion can be described in specific actions that allow us to consider any putative parallels, and so to note and confirm any innovation in comparison with the Jewish religious context in which devotion to Jesus erupted.

I have explored these matters for over thirty-five years now in a number of publications ranging from essays focused on this or that particular issue or bit of evidence to larger works, from my 1988 book, *One God, One Lord: Early Christian Devotion and Ancient Jewish Monotheism*, to my large 2003 volume, *Lord Jesus Christ: Devotion to Jesus in Earliest Christianity*, and subsequent studies.[1] In this book I draw on this body of work to emphasize how remarkable and significant the earliest expressions of devotion to Jesus were in their historical context. New Testament scholars (along with many other scholars of early Christianity) have often tended either to overlook the significance of worship, or have downplayed its importance in favor of a focus, almost entirely, on christological titles and other expressions of beliefs about Jesus. I grant the obvious importance of these, but, as I wish to show in what follows, I also want to underline the phenomena of earliest Christian worship, particularly the ways that the risen Jesus featured in worship.

---

1. My initial publication on this subject, "New Testament Christology: A Critique of Bousset's Influence," *Theological Studies* 40 (1979): 306–17, was a marker of my aim to make a fresh study of the origins of devotion to Jesus. The book-length studies that followed began with *One God, One Lord: Early Christian Devotion and Ancient Jewish Monotheism* (Philadelphia: Fortress Press; London: SCM, 1988; 2nd ed., Edinburgh: T&T Clark, 1998; 3rd ed., London: Bloomsbury T&T Clark, 2015), and continued with *At the Origins of Christian Worship: The Context and Character of Earliest Christian Devotion* (Grand Rapids: Eerdmans, 1999); *Lord Jesus Christ: Devotion to Jesus in Earliest Christianity* (Grand Rapids: Eerdmans, 2003); *How on Earth Did Jesus Become a God? Historical Questions about Earliest Devotion to Jesus* (Grand Rapids: Eerdmans, 2005); and *God in New Testament Theology* (Nashville: Abingdon, 2010).

THE PLAN OF THIS BOOK

I first briefly describe the scholarly context of the following discussion. I do not attempt anything close to an exhaustive catalog of scholars, but instead focus on key figures and key works that have been influential and/or that constitute noteworthy options, and with specific reference to the origins of the worship of Jesus.

Then, I begin my own case with a brief discussion demonstrating the centrality of worship in ancient religion. This is necessary because, especially in Western cultures, scholars and the general public have come to regard doctrines and confessional statements as the key expressions of religion, almost to the exclusion of anything else, and typically to the neglect of early Christian worship practices.

Thereafter, I introduce "ancient Jewish monotheism," which was expressed most directly and explicitly in a refusal to worship the many deities of the Roman period, confining worship to the one God of biblical tradition. I address both terminological issues and issues of substance, my main point being that Roman-era Judaism was known for the exclusivity of its worship. The one God alone was to be worshipped. This exclusivity, I contend, is the crucial historical context in which to perceive the significance of the devotional pattern characteristic of earliest circles of the Christian movement.

Next, I survey some key texts that reflect the major christological claims characteristic of earliest Christian circles. I concentrate on Paul's Letters in particular because, by common scholarly judgment, they preserve our earliest evidence of the beliefs about Jesus professed in the very first years, the key letters written roughly 50–60 CE.

I then turn to what is in fact the material that I most wish to emphasize, and that is the evidence of the kinds of devotional practices reflected in our earliest texts, particularly practices in which the risen Christ had a prominent place as joint recipient with God. I discuss specific practices and their significance in the context in which they first appeared. It is perhaps this emphasis on the specifics of earliest Christian devotion that is one of the contributions that I have tried to make over many years. I contend that the place of Jesus in earliest Christian devotional practice is the most remarkable feature of the young Christian movement, constituting what we may describe as a distinctive "mutation" in ancient Jewish tradition, a uniquely "dyadic" devotional pattern in which God and Jesus are recipients.

THE SCHOLARLY CONTEXT

Before I lay out my case for the nature and significance of earliest Jesus-devotion, I sketch here the scholarly context, focusing on key earlier and contemporary studies that primarily address historical questions about how Jesus came to be given the cultic devotion that is reflected already in Paul's Letters (our earliest Christian evidence).

Over the entire twentieth century, particularly influential were a group of scholars in Göttingen typically referred to as the *religionsgeschichtliche Schule* (history of religion school).[2] These included Hermann Gunkel, William Wrede, Ernst Troeltsch, Wilhelm Heitmüller, and Paul Wernle, all of whom were active in the early decades of the century. But probably the most well-known and influential member of this group was Wilhelm Bousset, and his most relevant publication was his book *Kyrios Christos: A History of Belief in Christ from the Beginnings of Christianity to Irenaeus*, which appeared initially in German

---

2. For fuller discussion, see, e.g., Werner Georg Kümmel, *The New Testament: The History of the Investigation of Its Problems*, trans. S. McLean Gilmour and Howard C. Kee (Nashville: Abingdon, 1972), 245–80.

in 1913. As the title indicates, it was a wide-ranging analysis of christological beliefs and devotional practice from the earliest moments after Jesus' execution down to the end of the second century CE. It remains an impressive piece of work, in breadth of coverage, in depth of engagement with the topic, and in the lively way that it was written. The English translation (made from the fifth German edition) was published much later, in 1970, which reflected the continuing importance of the book and the interest in it several decades after its initial appearance.[3]

A major factor in Bousset's subsequent influence was the strong affirmation of his book by Rudolf Bultmann, surely one of the most important New Testament scholars of the twentieth century. Bultmann had assisted in the preparation of the second edition of *Kyrios Christos* (1921), published after Bousset's untimely death. Bultmann also wrote a short introduction to the fifth German edition (1965), declaring, "Among the works of New Testament scholarship the study of which I used to recommend in my lectures to students as indispensable, above all belonged Wilhelm Bousset's *Kyrios Christos*."[4]

But from the outset, well before Bultmann's endorsement and long before the English translation, Bousset's book acquired a wide and powerful influence, effectively setting the agenda for all subsequent studies of the origins of devotion to Jesus. Already by 1917, Geerhardus Vos's essay "The *Kyrios Christos* Controversy" required sixty-eight pages to review the academic debate over the book to that point![5] The key issue in that debate was whether

---

3. The English translation, Wilhelm Bousset, *Kyrios Christos: A History of Belief in Christ from the Beginnings of Christianity to Irenaeus*, trans. John E. Steely (Nashville: Abingdon, 1970), was republished with a new introduction by me (Waco, TX: Baylor University Press, 2013), v–xx. In the ensuing discussion, my references are to this English translation.

4. Bousset, *Kyrios Christos*, 7.

5. Geerhardus Vos, "The *Kyrios Christos* Controversy," *PTR* 15 (1917): 21–89.

the origins of the worship of Jesus lay in Jewish circles of believers in Jerusalem, or, as Bousset contended, in diaspora settings
such as Antioch and Damascus, where he posited believers were
more subject to pagan influences in which divinized heroes and
multiple deities were more acceptable than in Roman Judea.
There were immediately major critiques in Germany, which
prompted Bousset to write a small monograph replying to his
critics.[6] Among English-language scholars as well, there were
critics, and at least two important lecture series delivered in
response to Bousset's book.

The book by J. Gresham Machen, *The Origin of Paul's Religion*,
sprang from his 1921 Sprunt Lectures at Union Theological
Seminary (Virginia), his aim being a critical engagement with
Bousset's work, particularly his view that Paul's religious
beliefs were shaped by "Hellenistic Christianity" and not by
the "primitive Christianity in Palestine."[7] A few years later, in
his Bampton Lectures, A. E. J. Rawlinson stated his intention "to
grapple constructively in English with the work of Bousset and
of other writers belonging to the so-called *religionsgeschichtliche*

---

6. German critiques included Paul Althaus, "Unser Herr Jesus: Eine neute-
setamentliche Untersuchung: Zur Auseinandersetzung mit W. Bousset," *Neue
Kirchliche Zeitschrift* 26 (1915): 439–57; Paul Wernle, "Jesus und Paulus: Antitheses
zu Bousset's *Kyrios Christos*," *Zeitschrift für Theologie und Kirche* 25 (1915): 1–92.
Bousset responded with *Jesus der Herr: Nachträge und Auseinandersetzungen zu
"Kyrios Christos,"* FRLANT n.s. 8 (Göttingen: Vandenhoeck & Ruprecht, 1916).

7. J. Gresham Machen, *The Origin of Paul's Religion* (London: Hodder &
Stoughton, 1921; repr., New York: Macmillan, 1925), 30. Machen's subsequent
involvement in church quarrels contributed to his marginalization in subsequent scholarship. But, though unavoidably dated in some matters, Machen's
book deserves more notice than it has received. He was prescient in some views
that have come to be associated with other scholars, e.g., his judgment that
"there is no evidence that before his conversion Paul was under real conviction
of sin" (65), a view now typically credited to Krister Stendahl's essay, "Paul and
the Introspective Conscience of the West," *Harvard Theological Review* 56 (1963):
199–215, republished in Stendahl, *Paul among Jews and Gentiles* (Philadelphia:
Fortress Press, 1976), 78–96.

Schule."[8] Rawlinson's critique was particularly remembered for his characterization of the Aramaic cry "Maranatha," in 1 Corinthians 16:22 as "the Achilles heel of the theory of Bousset," noting Bousset's varying attempts "to get rid of it."[9] Rawlinson's point was that, contra Bousset, this Aramaic phrase ("Our Lord, come"!) could only be taken as indicating that Jesus was addressed in cultic acclamation as "Lord," initially in Aramaic-speaking Jewish-Christian circles in Roman Judea, not only in diaspora locations more subject to pagan religious influences. Nevertheless, Bousset's book commanded wide assent well after its appearance, as reflected in the enthusiastic responses to the English translation in 1970.[10]

In an essay published in 1979, however, I laid out several important matters on which I contended that Bousset had been incorrect, and I argued that it was necessary to address the origins of the worship of Jesus again and on correct bases.[11] In subsequent publications, I have referred to Bousset's work both appreciatively and also with criticism.[12] Bousset was correct to identify

8. A. E. J. Rawlinson, *The New Testament Doctrine of Christ* (London: Longmans, Green, 1926), ix.

9. Rawlinson, *New Testament Doctrine of Christ,* 235, part of an appended note on the topic, 231–37.

10. See, e.g., Hendrikus Boers, "Jesus and Christian Faith: New Testament Christology since Bousset's *Kyrios Christos,*" *Journal of Biblical Literature* 89 (1970): 450–56; Norman Perrin, "Reflections on the Publication in English of Bousset's *Kyrios Christos,*" *Expository Times* 82 (1971): 340–42. As an example of Bousset's influence, Burton L. Mack, *A Myth of Innocence: Mark and Christian Origins* (Philadelphia: Fortress Press, 1988), posited anonymous circles of Christians in Syria, among whom the "Christ cult" supposedly originated; these circles sharply differentiated from the original followers of Jesus in Roman Judea, for whom Jesus was only an inspiring teacher.

11. Hurtado, "New Testament Christology," 306–17.

12. In addition to my introduction to the republication of the English translation of *Kyrios Christos* noted earlier, see Larry W. Hurtado, "Christ-Devotion in the First Two Centuries: Reflections and a Proposal," *Toronto Journal of Theology*

what he called the "Kyrios cult," the treatment of the risen Jesus as recipient of worship, as the most important phenomenon to investigate. But he was incorrect in claiming that this could not have emerged in an authentically Jewish context, and instead only in a setting where pagan religious influences operated.

Bousset was also correct to acknowledge that the worship of Jesus erupted early, so early that it was the form of early Christian faith that the young Pharisee Saul of Tarsus had initially opposed and then subsequently embraced. That is, even on Bousset's reckoning, the "Kyrios cult" emerged within the first few months or years at most after Jesus' execution. On the chronological issue, thus, I view Bousset as much closer to the truth than some subsequent scholars such as J. D. G. Dunn and Maurice Casey (engaged later in this work) who have contended that the worship of Jesus only emerged in the late first century, and did not characterize the devotional practices of Paul and his churches.[13]

As to the chronological issue, in my view, one of the most important essays of the late twentieth century for the study of Christian origins was Martin Hengel's "Christology and New Testament Chronology."[14] For Hengel showed concisely but

---

12 (1996): 17–33; Hurtado, "Wilhelm Bousset's *Kyrios Christos*: An Appreciative and Critical Assessment." *Early Christianity* 6 (2015): 1–13.

13. See, e.g., Maurice Casey, *From Jewish Prophet to Gentile God: The Origins and Development of New Testament Christology* (Louisville: Westminster John Knox, 1991); James D. G. Dunn, *Did the First Christians Worship Jesus? The New Testament Evidence* (Louisville: Westminster John Knox, 2010).

14. Hengel's essay originally appeared in German, "Christologie und neutestamentliche Chronologie: Zu einer Aporie in der Geschichte des Urchristentums" in *Neues Testament und Geschichte, Festschrift O. Cullmann*, ed. Heinrich Baltensweiler and Bo Reicke (Zurich: Theologischer Verlag, 1972), 43–67, and was a key influence on my own thinking from the 1970s onward. The English translation appeared in Martin Hengel, *Between Jesus and Paul: Studies in the Earliest History of Christianity* (London: SCM, 1983), "Christology and New Testament Chronology," 30–47, and I cite it in this discussion.

cogently that the textual evidence did not allow for the sorts of elaborate and multistage developments in earliest Christian circles that have sometimes been posited.[15] As Hengel (and also Bousset) noted, already in Paul's undisputed letters, dated around 50–60 CE, the earliest extant Christian texts, we see a developed devotional pattern in which Jesus is invoked and acclaimed as the "Lord" of the gathered worship circle, the agent of God's creation of the world, and the uniquely exalted figure to whom all of creation is to give obeisance. Moreover, in these letters these things are not so much taught as they are presumed as already familiar to Paul's intended readers. In Hengel's words, "The time between the death of Jesus and the fully developed Christology which we find in the earliest Christian documents, the letters of Paul, is so short that the development which takes place within it can only be called amazing."[16] The elapsed time in question is a scant twenty years.

But, we must also note (1) that Paul was "converted" from opponent to enthusiastic proponent of the Jesus movement within only a year or two at most after Jesus' death (as Bousset had agreed), (2) that the Jesus-devotion reflected in Paul's Letters is most likely the stance that he had previously opposed and then came to embrace at that early point, and (3) that Paul persistently underscored and sought to maintain links with the *Jerusalem church and its leadership*, not with Antioch or other diaspora centers. These all lead to the conclusion that the historical development in question, the treatment of Jesus as the "cult Lord" rightfully entitled to the sort of reverence otherwise confined to God, was amazingly early and explosively rapid,

---

15. E.g., "Palestinian Jewish," "Hellenistic Jewish," "Hellenistic gentile" stages, all sometimes placed within the first several decades of the first century, and a distinguishable Christology posited for each.

16. Hengel, "Christology and New Testament Chronology," 31.

not an incremental process. To cite Hengel's memorable characterization of the time span of the approximately eighteen
years between Jesus' death and the earliest of Paul's letters,
"In essentials more happened in christology within these few
years than in the whole subsequent seven hundred years of
church history."[17]

The key point to take from the foregoing is that the risen/
exalted Jesus became the recipient of cultic devotion and was
lauded in remarkable christological claims from within the
very earliest years after his crucifixion. The point of difference
between the presentation of matters by Bousset on the one hand
and the view of others such as Hengel and myself is whether this
development could have emerged initially in circles of Jewish
believers in Roman Judea. But, to underscore the point, even in
Bousset's scheme the emergence of devotion to Jesus as Kyrios
of the worship-gathering was astonishingly early. Further, to
reiterate another point made earlier, Bousset and others, including those who disagreed on other matters, agreed that this cultic
devotion to Jesus was momentous—indeed, the most significant
development in the early Christian movement.

In addition to his emphasis on the chronological issue,
Hengel also made other important contributions to the study
of early christological issues. His little volume, *Son of God*,
remains an incisive analysis of the origins and early significance of beliefs about Jesus' divine sonship.[18] In several other
studies, Hengel also drew attention to the important role of

---

17. Hengel, "Christology and New Testament Chronology," 39–40.

18. Martin Hengel, *The Son of God: The Origin of Christology and the History of Jewish-Hellenistic Religion* (Philadelphia: Fortress Press, 1976).

Spirit-inspired "odes/hymns" as vehicles for early christological claims and convictions, these typically expressed within worship settings.[19]

In addition to Hengel, another of the most important figures in the contemporary discussion of the origins of Jesus-devotion is Richard Bauckham. In an essay published several decades ago, Bauckham pointed to the importance of the worship of Jesus in early Christian circles, noting that this sat alongside a firm stance otherwise that only God should be worshipped.[20] I consider this essay one of the most important in the contemporary scene. Loren Stuckenbruck took up Bauckham's analysis and extended it, arriving at basically a similar view, that the various prohibitions against worshipping other beings (including angels) in Jewish texts make the inclusion of Jesus as a recipient of worship along with God in early Christian texts an apparently novel development.[21]

In more recent publications, however, Bauckham has emphasized conceptual or doctrinal developments, specifically proposing that in earliest christological thought Jesus was included within what Bauckham calls "the divine identity."[22] Moreover,

---

19. Martin Hengel, "Hymns and Christology," in *Between Jesus and Paul*, 78–96; Hengel, *Studies in Early Christology* (Edinburgh: T&T Clark, 1995), esp. 227–91.

20. Richard J. Bauckham, "The Worship of Jesus in Apocalyptic Christianity," *New Testament Studies* 27 (1981): 322–41. In a subsequent book, Bauckham produced an expanded version of this essay: "The Worship of Jesus," in *The Climax of Prophecy: Studies on the Book of Revelation* (Edinburgh: T&T Clark, 1993), 118–49.

21. Loren T. Stuckenbruck, *Angel Veneration and Christology*, WUNT 2/70 (Tübingen: J. C. B. Mohr [Siebeck], 1995). Stuckenbruck proposed, however, that what he called "venerative language" about angels in Jewish texts may have some significance, although he granted that it did not amount to the worship of angels.

22. Richard Bauckham, *God Crucified: Monotheism and Christology in the New Testament* (Carlisle, UK: Paternoster, 1998); republished with additional material as *Jesus and the God of Israel: God Crucified and Other Studies on the New Testament's Christology of Divine Identity* (Milton Keynes, UK: Paternoster, 2008).

he now seems to make the worship of Jesus a corollary of this view of Jesus. That is, Bauckham appears to make the worship of Jesus an early consequence of the specific beliefs that Jesus shares the divine throne and the divine action of creation of the worlds. Bauckham correctly points to the remarkable christological beliefs evident in earliest texts. But I find scant indication in earliest Christian texts that the worship of Jesus was a logical step taken as a consequence of these christological beliefs. Instead, it seems to me that the dyadic devotional pattern that we see in these early texts was a direct response to what believers saw as God's express demand, likely conveyed via powerful religious experiences that struck recipients as revelations of God's will.[23] In my view, the worship of Jesus was not a corollary of something else, but was a noteworthy development in its own right that arose as obedience to the perception that it was God's will.

In the current scholarly context, however, over against those who posit that the worship of Jesus erupted in the earliest circles of believers, some notable voices contend that the worship of Jesus arose much later, only in the latter decades of the first century CE. Prominent among these is Dunn, who judges that Jesus is not really given worship in Paul's Letters, although Dunn allows that in the later decades of the first century CE we do see something that looks like the worship of Jesus, as reflected in Revelation 5, for example.[24] But Dunn argues that, in the main,

---

23. See my discussion of Bauckham's views in "Worship and Divine Identity: Richard Bauckham's Christological Pilgrimage," in *In the Fullness of Time: Essays on Christology, Creation, and Eschatology in Honor of Richard Bauckham*, ed. Daniel M. Gurner, Grant Macaskill, and Jonathan T. Pennington (Grand Rapids: Eerdmans, 2016), 82–96. I discuss the importance of revelatory religious experiences later in the present study.

24. Dunn, *Did the First Christians Worship Jesus?*, 130–32. See my review at *Larry Hurtado's Blog*, https://larryhurtado.files.wordpress.com/2010/07/

"the first Christians did not think of Jesus as to be worshipped in and for himself . . . as wholly God, or fully identified with God, far less as a god." Instead, Dunn insists, they worshipped God "in and through" Jesus and worshipped "Jesus-in-God and God-in-Jesus."[25]

On the one hand, Dunn is obviously correct. In the New Testament writings, Jesus was not worshipped as another deity alongside God; and for early believers Jesus did not rival or replace God. Instead, typically in early Christian texts Jesus was reverenced in, and on account of, his relationship to the one God, for example, as the unique Son of God, Word of God, and image of God. But that is just as true for Revelation and most other early Christian writings as for Paul! In Revelation 5, for example, "the Lamb" (the exalted Jesus) is worshipped as the one who was slain and "purchased for God" people from every nation (v. 9); and in the final verses the Lamb is hymned along with God "who sits on the throne" (v. 13).

On the other hand, as we will see later in this discussion, from Paul's Letters onward the risen Jesus was given the kinds of reverence that align remarkably with the ways that God was reverenced. To be sure, Jesus was not worshipped as a second deity or apart from God "the Father" (and yet that seems to be

---

dunn-was-jesus-worshipped-review.pdf. Dunn's former PhD student James F. McGrath has argued somewhat similarly in *The Only True God: Early Christian Monotheism in Its Jewish Context* (Urbana: University of Illinois Press, 2009). See my review at *Larry Hurtado's Blog*, https://larryhurtado.files.wordpress.com/2010/07/mcgrath-reveiw-essay1.pdf. Maurice Casey likewise contended in *From Jewish Prophet to Gentile God* that Jesus acquired a divine status only late in the first century, in the circles of believers reflected in the Gospel of John. Casey attributed this to the influx of large numbers of non-Jewish converts whose pagan background allegedly made them more ready to deify Jesus. In my view, his case suffers a similar problem as Dunn's in failing to take adequate account of the data of Paul's Letters, which reflect a robust dyadic devotional pattern already taken as typical of believers by the 50s.

25. Dunn, Did the First Christians Worship Jesus?, 146.

what Dunn requires for Jesus to have been worshipped). But in Paul's Letters as well as subsequent early Christian writings the worship pattern has a clear "dyadic" shape, in which the risen Jesus is included uniquely along with God as recipient of the kinds of reverence that can only be understood as worship. This dyadic pattern of worship is the novel development that is unparalleled in the wider Jewish tradition of the time, and that justifies attention.

In attempting to account for this, Adela Yarbro Collins proposed the influence of Roman-era ruler cults.[26] But to my mind her proposal requires us to imagine this influence in Judea and among devout Jews, an appropriation of pagan religious notions for which we have no other example in Jewish tradition of the time. Indeed, what evidence we have of Jewish attitudes toward Roman emperor worship reflects utter disdain.[27] A conscious appropriation of ruler cult among earliest circles of Jewish believers therefore seems to me too much of an imaginative leap to be taken seriously. And her other suggestion that it all may have been an unconscious move seems to me no less fanciful. How would early believers unconsciously borrow their basic religious ideas from a religious practice that they regarded with horror?

------

26. Adela Yarbro Collins, "The Worship of Jesus and the Imperial Cult," in *The Jewish Roots of Christological Monotheism: Papers From the St. Andrews Conference on the Historical Origins of the Worship of Jesus*, ed. Carey C. Newman, James R. Davila, and Gladys S. Lewis (Leiden: Brill, 1999), 234–57; and more recently, Collins, "'How on Earth Did Jesus Become a God?': A Reply," in *Israel's God and Rebecca's Children: Christology and Community in Early Judaism and Christianity*, ed. David B. Capes et al. (Waco, TX: Baylor University Press, 2007), 55–66. Michael Peppard laid out a somewhat similar view: *The Son of God in the Roman World: Divine Sonship in Its Social and Political Context* (New York: Oxford University Press, 2011); but see my review essay, "The 'Son of God' in/and the Roman Empire: A Review Essay," *Larry Hurtado's Blog*, January 7, 2013, https://larryhurtado.word-press.com/2013/01/17/the-son-of-god-inand-the-roman-empire-a-review-essay/.

27. See, e.g., Philo of Alexandria, *Embassy to Gaius*.

Another contribution in the contemporary scholarly debate about the origins of the worship of Jesus is from Crispin Fletcher-Louis. In an earlier essay, he contended that ancient Jewish tradition included the idea that God could be directly represented in a human figure who was, thus, entitled to worship.[28] More recently, he has published the first of a projected multi-volume work further affirming this and also intended to lay out programmatically his own approach to the question of the origins of Jesus-devotion.[29] With only the introductory volume to this project available, it is possible here only to engage briefly what seem to be his basic contentions. In my view, the key problem with his position is that (as he admits) there is no evidence that in Second Temple Jewish tradition any other human figure was accorded the kinds of reverence given to the exalted Jesus in early Christian circles. That is, there is no indication that the putative idea that it was appropriate to worship the human embodiment of God generated any other example of the dyadic devotional pattern that we see reflected in the New Testament. So, even if we grant this supposed idea (and it is not so clear to me that we should), it was not sufficient to generate the worship of Jesus, and something else must be sought to account for that novel dyadic devotional pattern.

Fletcher-Louis seems to recognize this problem, and he now invokes a further claim (to be defended more fully in subsequent volumes in his project) that the actual catalyst for the worship

28. Crispin H. T. Fletcher-Louis, "The Worship of Divine Humanity as God's Image and the Worship of Jesus," in Newman, Davila, and Lewis, *Jewish Roots*, 112–28.

29. Crispin Fletcher-Louis, *Jesus Monotheism*, vol. 1, *Christological Origins: The Emerging Consensus and Beyond* (Eugene, OR: Cascade, 2015). See reviews by me, *RBL* (August 2016): https://www.bookreviews.org/pdf/10588_11764.pdf; and Blake Jurgens, *RBL* (June 2017): https://www.bookreviews.org/pdf/10588_11827.pdf.

of Jesus in early Christian circles was Jesus' own teaching about his person. That is, in his most recent work Fletcher-Louis proposes that Jesus knew himself to be the human embodiment of God, and so worthy of worship, and taught this to his disciples, although they seem not to have acted on this until after Jesus' death and resurrection.

As attractive as Fletcher-Louis's proposal might be for some theologically, allowing them to base the worship of Jesus on Jesus' own teaching, there are problems that make it dubious on historical grounds. For example, although the Gospel of John features Jesus expressing his heavenly origins and divine status (e.g., John 5:17–24; 6:35–40; 17:5), the Synoptic Gospels do not. So it seems to most scholars that the Gospel of John reflects an account of Jesus that is overtly refracted through the elevated view of him that erupted in the "post-Easter" setting.[30]

But the major problem is that the earliest Christian texts do not base the worship of Jesus on his instructions or demands but, instead, on the actions of God in raising Jesus from death and exalting him to heavenly glory (e.g., Phil 2:9–11). That is, these texts justify the worship of Jesus as the obedient response to God's glorification of Jesus of Nazareth, and God's requirement that Jesus should be reverenced accordingly. In the aftermath of Jesus' resurrection, earliest believers quickly came to ascribe to Jesus a "preexistence" and an "incarnation" (e.g., Phil 2:6–8), but these concepts seem to have been corollaries of their prior conviction that God had raised Jesus from death and designated him as "Messiah and Lord" (e.g., Acts 2:36; 17:30–31). In short, it is unlikely that during his earthly ministry Jesus taught his

---

30. See, e.g., my essay, "Remembering and Revelation: The Historic and Glorified Jesus in the Gospel of John," in Capes et al., *Israel's God*, 195–213.

disciples that he was the incarnation of a preexistent Son/Word, and that he was worthy of worship.

Among contemporary publications, probably the best-selling recent book on the origins of Christology is by Bart Ehrman.[31] On some points, Ehrman simply echoes the findings of other scholars, such as the judgment that the worship of Jesus erupted in the earliest circles of believers. But Ehrman also proffers a few problematic views of his own, such as the notion that Paul thought of Jesus as an angelic being, that angels were worshipped in Jewish circles, and so Jesus was worshipped. No part of this has any real basis in the evidence, however, as I have pointed out in my reviews of Ehrman's book.

From the foregoing very brief discussion, it should be apparent that the origins of Christology and in particular the worship of Jesus remain subjects of intense scholarly interest and debate. In addition to those works discussed above, there are a number of others that deserve at least mentioning. These include David Capes's study of Old Testament "Yahweh texts" applied to Jesus, Carey Newman's analysis of Paul's "glory Christology," and others.[32] My own body of work over several decades comprises my efforts to address these subjects in historical terms, and I refer interested readers to these publications for a fuller presentation

---

31. Bart D. Ehrman, *How Jesus Became God: The Exaltation of a Jewish Preacher From Galilee* (New York: HarperOne, 2014). See my blog posting on the book, "How Jesus Became 'God,' per Ehrman," *Larry Hurtado's Blog*, May 29, 2014, https://larryhurtado.wordpress.com/2014/05/29/how-jesus-became-god-per-ehrman/, and my published review, "Lord and God," *The Christian Century*, August 6, 2014, 26–28 (included in the appendix of this book).

32. David B. Capes, *Old Testament Yahweh Texts in Paul's Christology*, WUNT 2/47 (Tübingen: J. C. B. Mohr [Paul Siebeck], 1992); Carey C. Newman, *Paul's Glory-Christology: Tradition and Rhetoric*, NovTSup 69 (Leiden: Brill, 1992). Note also, e.g., Larry J. Kreitzer, *Jesus and God in Paul's Eschatology*, JSNTSup 19 (Sheffield: JSOT Press, 1987); Carl J. Davis, *The Name and Way of the Lord*, JSNTSup 129 (Sheffield: JSOT Press, 1996).

of my views. In the following pages, I focus on the significance
of the devotional practices reflected in earliest Christian texts
in the context of worship in the larger Roman-era context.

CHAPTER 2

WORSHIP IN THE ANCIENT WORLD

For various historical reasons, most of us shaped by Christian tradition (at least in the West) have likely come to think that the key expression of one's religiousness and religious stance is a confessional statement, a creed, a series of propositions stating beliefs. Certainly Christians have invested considerable energies in developing confessional statements and working out theological themes over a long time. Think of the Apostles' Creed or the Nicene Creed, or the many subsequent creedal statements that have defined, and often divided, Christian groups and denominations down the centuries.

Especially in the Protestant Reformation and on into the seventeenth century, agreement in confessional statements tended to dictate whether people were extended Christian fellowship or were shunned, or even put to death. Indeed, agreement in details was required, not simply basics. For example, think of the bitter disputations and mutual shunning connected with differences over how to express the religious significance of the Eucharist. Whether you confessed "real presence," "transubstantiation," or one of the other theological formulas of the time could determine whether you were treated as a fellow believer or a heretic. Indeed, most Christian circles of the time insisted on agreement on how you understood the Eucharist as a condition for sharing it. Odd, is it not? Participation in this core ritual supposed to be emblematic of Christian fellowship was made to depend, not on being baptized and the Christian profession of faith, but on agreement in this or that theological formulation about *how* Eucharist was to be understood!

And, of course, subsequently, differences over sometimes quite intricate issues of theology have been the basis for mutual shunning. I have heard of "five-point" Calvinists rejecting "three-point" Calvinists! Effectively, everything depended on full agreement to a set of confessional statements. In short, the dominant view has been that doctrine was crucial and the core of a religion, and worship a mere corollary of doctrine.

But in the ancient Roman world, things were different.[1] What we would call "religion" was mainly ritual actions, particularly sacrifice.[2] Of course, there were beliefs too. For example, people obviously had to believe that gods existed and that they would respond to the right sort of petition as a premise for engaging in those ritual actions. But, for the most part, religious beliefs

---

1. For an excellent and wide-ranging survey of Roman-era religion, see Mary Beard, John North, and Simon Price, *Religions of Rome*, 2 vols. (Cambridge: Cambridge University Press, 1998).

2. Note, however, Brent Nongbri, *Before Religion: A History of a Modern Concept* (New Haven: Yale University Press, 2013), who shows how the modern term and concept of "religion" as a discrete activity developed.

were more implicit and not foregrounded in the way that beliefs came to be in Christian tradition.[3]

Moreover, in general, the various deities of the Roman world had little to say about daily behavior or "ethics," the principal exception being the Jewish deity and the many commandments in his Torah. But for most "pagans," teaching about "ethics" was more the province of philosophy, not religion.[4] Instead of doctrines or behavioral teachings, we could say that it was what deities you worshipped and the nature of the worship that you practiced that defined you religiously. In short, "cultic practice," especially sacrifice, the equivalent of what we mean by "worship," was typically the heart of Roman-era religion.[5]

People of the time approached the traditional deities generally because they needed some divine help, and the usual practice was to offer or promise the deity in question some gift in anticipation of, or return for, answering the prayer for that help.[6] This is reflected in the many *ex voto* objects found in ancient pagan shrines. These were typically small physical items given to the deity/temple as an expression of thanks. For example, if the deity healed your foot, you might offer the deity's

3. Charles King, "The Organization of Roman Religious Beliefs," *Classical Antiquity* 22 (2003): 275–312.

4. See, e.g., my discussion of this matter in my book, *Destroyer of the Gods: Early Christian Distinctiveness in the Roman World* (Waco, TX: Baylor University Press, 2016), chap. 5.

5. But Roman-era "cultic practice" was more typically petition and/or thanks for answered petition rather than adoration or "worship" as it came to be known in Christian tradition. See, e.g., M. P. Nilsson, "Pagan Divine Service in Late Antiquity," *Harvard Theological Review* 38 (1945): 63–69; Royden Keith Yerkes, *Sacrifice in Greek and Roman Religions and Early Judaism* (London: Black, 1953).

6. E.g., John Pinsent, "Roman Spirituality," in *Classical Mediterranean Spirituality*, ed. A. H. Armstrong (New York: Crossroad, 1986), 154–94; Ramsay MacMullen, *Paganism in the Roman Empire* (New Haven: Yale University Press, 1981); Javier Teixidor, *The Pagan God: Popular Religion in the Graeco-Roman Near East* (Princeton: Princeton University Press, 1977).

shrine a small replica of a foot (along with a sacrificial offering, of course). These objects were produced by local craftsmen and available for sale to those who visited shrines and temples.

There were also the scheduled rituals in honor of the traditional guardian deities of the various cities, and even rituals acknowledging the household deities seen as protectors of the family. In the Roman period that is our focus here, there were also rituals devoted to rulers, initially deceased Roman emperors, and then also the living emperor.[7] As reflected in the title of a lively account of Roman-era religion, it was "a world full of gods."[8]

Indeed, we could also say that cultic practice (worship) was how you affirmed the reality and validity of a deity. So, to refuse to reverence a deity was an offense against the deity, even an act of impiety, and was effectively to deny the deity's reality. Moreover, in the eyes of many people of the time, refusing to honor the gods might provoke them to retaliate, or at least to take offense. Offended city deities might not protect the city from plague, for example, and offended family deities might not protect the household from disease or other perils.

In the Roman era, consequently, a refusal to worship the gods could generate hostility, and even charges of impiety and atheism.[9] Early Christians often suffered hostility for their

---

7. Among the many works on worship of Roman emperors, e.g., S. R. F. Price, *Rituals and Power: The Roman Imperial Cult in Asia Minor* (Cambridge: Cambridge University Press, 1984); Fergus Millar, *The Emperor in the Roman World, 31 B.C.–A.D. 337* (Ithaca, NY: Cornell University Press, 1977); Jeffrey Brodd and Jonathan L. Reed, eds., *Rome and Religion: A Cross-Disciplinary Dialogue on the Imperial Cult* (Atlanta: Society of Biblical Literature, 2011).

8. Keith Hopkins, *A World Full of Gods: Pagans, Jews, and Christians in the Roman Empire* (London: Weidenfeld & Nicolson, 1999).

9. Anders B. Drachmann, *Atheism in Pagan Antiquity* (London: Gyldendal, 1922); Jan N. Bremmer, "Atheism in Antiquity," in *The Cambridge Companion to*

refusal to honor the gods, and were sometimes even accused of atheism for precisely this reason.[10] Indeed, the refusal to take part in sacrifice to the various deities of the Roman world was probably the most offensive feature of the early Christian movement. The second-century pagan critic of early Christianity Celsus expressed a readiness to overlook everything else that he found strange about Christians if only they would relent in their refusal to honor the traditional gods.[11] Philosophers of that period sometimes discussed and debated the nature of the gods, and whether they cared for humans, but what mattered was whether you joined in worshipping them. Even those philosophers who expressed doubts about the gods tended to continue to take part in the public rituals in honor of them. There is no indication that philosophical discussions about the gods were intended to have any major impact on the religious practices of the general populace.

For, to underscore the point again, the gods collectively were seen as the guardians of households, cities, nations, even the Roman Empire itself. Honoring the gods (again, especially by sacrifice), thus, was how people sought to ensure divine protection against such dangers as plague, and the gods' beneficence in such things as the supply of food, health, safe delivery of children, and other matters. To refuse to honor them, therefore,

---

Atheism, ed. Michael Martin (Cambridge: Cambridge University Press, 2007), 11–26.

10. E.g., the depiction of the cry of the pagan crowd, "Away with the atheists!" in *Martyrdom of Polycarp* 3.2.

11. The main body of the text of Celsus's critique, *The True Word*, is recoverable from the response to it written later by Origen. A translation is available in Henry Chadwick, trans., *Origen: Contra Celsum* (Cambridge: Cambridge University Press, 1965). See my discussion of pagan criticism of early Christians in my book *Destroyer of the Gods*, 20–36, and early Christianity as "a new kind of faith," 37–76; and also the fuller discussion by Robert L. Wilken, *The Christians as the Romans Saw Them* (New Haven: Yale University Press, 1984).

was impious, irresponsible, and even antisocial, for it potentially endangered the family, city, or the larger society. You did not have to ensure that you worshipped all the various deities by observing some sort of checklist; but you were expected to join freely in the worship of any deity when the occasion presented itself. It would certainly have been considered strange to refuse to do so.

Of course, Christians were not the first ones to get into trouble over refusing to worship the pagan gods. Indeed, the early Christian stance was simply a continuation of the cultic exclusivity that characterized Roman-era Judaism, the matrix in which the early Christian movement first emerged. Indicative of this, and indicative also of the importance of cultic practice in the ancient world, note the stories of Jewish resistance to Seleucid efforts to assimilate Jews as related in 1 Maccabees. In 2:15-28, officers of the Seleucid king come to the town of Modein in the Jewish homeland to "enforce apostasy" by persuading Jews to offer sacrifice "according to the king's command" (which probably means sacrifice to the pagan king's favored deity). Mattathias refuses, insisting that neither he nor his sons will abandon their ancestral "religion" (v. 22, the translation used in the NRSV). But the Greek word translated "religion" here is *latreia* (service), which in this context refers to worship practice, the (sacrificial) worship of the God of Israel counterposed here against the worship of the Seleucid deity. For in the story when another Jew complies with the demand of the king's officer and offers sacrifice on the pagan altar (v. 23), Mattathias kills both that fellow Jew and the officer, tears down the pagan altar, and summons "everyone who is zealous for the law and supports the covenant" to join him in the ensuing revolt (vv. 24-28). Likewise, in the accounts of the Maccabean martyrs the demand put to them is not to sign a confessional statement, but to take part in pagan sacrifice (e.g., 2 Macc 6:18-7:2). In short, Jews and pagans were agreed on at least this one point, that what counted as what we would call "religion" was cultic honor (sacrifice) to a deity. For devout Jews of the time, their worship of God was to be exclusive, and so sacrifice to the other deities was "idolatry," a matter to which I return in the next chapter. For pagans, this exclusivity and refusal to honor the gods was a particularly objectionable, even antisocial, feature of Judaism.

Somewhat similarly to these stories of the Maccabean period, Pliny (the early second-century Roman governor of Pontus and Bithynia), in his report of his handling of those denounced to him as Christians, says that he required them to recite a prayer to the pagan gods, make supplication with incense and wine to Caesar's image, and to curse Christ. Note that these are all ritual actions, even the verbal cursing of Christ, and performing them is what indicated whether those accused conformed to the established religious stance.[12]

So, to underscore the point, in the ancient setting worship/ritual practice was the key expression of "religion," and doctrines or beliefs were generally more an implicit (or even an irrelevant) matter. To appreciate earliest Christianity intelligently, we have to understand the primacy of worship practice in defining what "religion" was then in the Roman world. Developments or differences in worship practice could be of major importance. In a truly historical approach to early

---

12. For text and commentary on this and Pliny's other letters, see A. N. Sherwin-White, *The Letters of Pliny: A Historical and Social Commentary* (Oxford: Clarendon, 1966). For my own discussion of Pliny, see *Destroyer of the Gods,* 22–26. The stories of early Christian martyrs reinforce the centrality of sacrifice: e.g., the *Martyrdom of Sts. Perpetua and Felicitas.* The third-century certificates of sacrifice issued under Emperor Decius (249–51 CE) also reflect this. For a handy collection of texts on the relations between early Christianity and the Roman world, see J. Stevenson, ed., *A New Eusebius* (London: SPCK, 1974).

Christianity, worship practices must be a central matter, and not sidelined or relegated to a place of secondary importance.

CHAPTER 3

ANCIENT JEWISH MONOTHEISM

It is important to note that in the Roman era, every nation had its own gods, and people of whatever nation generally accepted the validity of the gods of other nations. All the gods of all the nations were generally regarded as valid and worthy of worship.[1] So if you traveled abroad, you might readily join in ceremonies in honor of the gods of foreign lands, as well as those in honor of your own gods. There was no notion that your gods would be offended if you joined in honoring the deities of other cities or nations. The key exception, however, was the behavior typical of Jews.

As I have noted, those who identified themselves as Jews typically confined worship firmly to their own singular deity, and they regarded the worship of other gods as "idolatry." That

---

1. There were some traditionalist Romans, however, who objected to foreign gods and cults gaining a foothold in the city of Rome. But they had no objection to the worship of foreign gods in foreign lands.

term itself (Greek: *eidōlolatria*, "religious service to an idol," a curious term that seems to have originated in Jewish usage) expresses the disdain with which Jews regarded the deities of other peoples. Obviously, pagans did not think of their own gods as "idols" or their worship as "idolatry"! For the term "idol" (Greek: *eidōlon*) signifies something that is a phantom or a mere image of the mind; and "idolatry" thus designates the worship of an illusory thing, or at least something that is not a valid recipient of worship. I emphasize, however, that the issue for Jews was not whether the pagan gods *existed*, but instead that it was wrong to *worship* them. Jews (and Christians as well) were often ready to acknowledge that the pagan gods were real beings (albeit evil beings), but the point was that these beings were unworthy as recipients of worship, which was to be reserved for the one God alone.

This exclusivity in worship practice is what I mean by referring to "ancient Jewish monotheism." But I need to clarify a precise terminological point. For the term "monotheism" has come in for a bit of critique. Scholars have rightly objected that, as defined in most dictionaries, "monotheism" means the belief that only one deity *exists*, and so it is inappropriate as a description of ancient Jews or Christians.[2] As I have noted, it is clear that ancient Jews (and subsequently Christians as well) were not so concerned to deny that pagan deities existed altogether. Indeed, in some Jewish and early Christian texts pagan deities are referred to as actual demons or fallen angels who have led

---

2. E.g., Peter Hayman, "Monotheism: A Misused Word in Jewish Studies?," *Journal of Jewish Studies* 42 (1991): 1–15; Paula Fredriksen, "Mandatory Retirement: Ideas in the Study of Christian Origins Whose Time Has Come to Go," *Studies in Religion/Sciences Religieuses* 35 (2006): 231–46, republished in *Israel's God and Rebecca's Children: Christology and Community in Early Judaism and Christianity; Essays in Honor of Larry W. Hurtado and Alan F. Segal*, ed. David B. Capes et al. (Waco, TX: Baylor University Press, 2007), 25–38.

the nations astray in treating them as gods, that is, recipients of worship. Jews, in other words, often seem to have accepted that the pagan gods were, or reflected, real beings. That was not the issue. Instead, it was their validity as recipients of worship that was the issue. Note, for example, Paul's statements in 1 Corinthians 10:19–21.

> What do I imply then? That food offered to idols is anything, or that an idol is anything? No, I imply that what pagans sacrifice they offer to demons and not to God. I do not want you to be partners with demons. You cannot drink the cup of the Lord and the cup of demons. You cannot partake of the table of the Lord and the table of demons.[3]

So, in relation to the terminology question, as I have proposed earlier in a journal article, although the dictionary definition of "monotheism" does not apply well to the ancient world, I think that we can refer to *"ancient Jewish* monotheism" as a handy designation for the firm cultic exclusivity that was typical of Roman-era Jewish tradition.[4] Some may prefer "ancient

---

3. Paul reflects here inherited Jewish attitudes toward pagan deities, as in LXX Deut 32:17; LXX Ps 95:5; LXX Isa 65:3. Note also, e.g., Jub. 22.16–17; 1 En. 99.7. But he also reflects the distinctive "mutation" in Jewish cultic practice that characterized the early Christian movement. For the "Lord" in Paul's statement whose cup and table demand an exclusivity is obviously the risen/exalted Lord Jesus.

4. This is not modern "monotheism" (as defined in dictionaries), but, instead, *"ancient Jewish* monotheism," and this was exhibited mainly in an exclusivity in cultic practice, Jews confining their worship to the one God. See Larry W. Hurtado, "'Ancient Jewish Monotheism' in the Hellenistic and Roman Periods," *Journal of Ancient Judaism* 4 (2013): 379–400; and my earlier discussion in "First Century Jewish Monotheism," *Journal for the Study of the New Testament* 71 (1998): 3–26, republished in my book, *How on Earth Did Jesus Become a God? Historical Questions about Earliest Devotion to Jesus* (Grand Rapids: Eerdmans, 2005), 111–33.

Jewish monolatry" or "henotheism" or some other label to cap-
ture the cultic exclusivity characteristic of ancient Jewish tradition. But whatever the label, it is this cultic exclusivity that
is clearly attested and crucial, both for understanding ancient
Judaism and for appreciating the historical significance of
Jesus-devotion.

Of course, from the Hellenistic period onward Jews were
often quite ready to adopt features of, and assimilate in some
matters to, Greek culture.[5] Greek language, for example,
appears to have gained widespread usage among Jews in diaspora locations and also in the Jewish homeland.[6] To cite another
example of the appropriation of Hellenistic culture, Jews generally also adopted the Greek custom of reclining in formal dining
occasions such as the Passover meal. In diaspora locations, Jews
sometimes even went so far as to make donations to pagan temples and made other gestures of respect for pagan deities, likely
to promote goodwill and acceptance of Jews by the wider civic
population. Jews such as Philo of Alexandria, who appears to
have undergone a Greek education, would have had to partic-
ipate (or at least acquiesce) in some gestures of reverence to

---

5. Among studies of Jewish engagement with the wider Greco-Roman cul-
ture, see John M. G. Barclay, *Jews in the Mediterranean Diaspora: From Alexander to
Trajan (323 BCE–117 CE)* (Edinburgh: T&T Clark, 1996); Erich S. Gruen, *Diaspora:
Jews Amidst Greeks and Romans* (Cambridge, MA: Harvard University Press, 2002).
The work often cited as the landmark study, however, is Martin Hengel, *Judaism
and Hellenism: Studies in the Encounter in Palestine During the Early Hellenistic
Period*, 2 vols. (London: SCM, 1974), which showed that the influence of Greek
language and culture was just as present in the Jewish homeland as in "dias-
pora" locations. See also his later volume *The "Hellenization" of Judaea in the First
Century After Christ* (London: SCM, 1989).

6. Among the many studies of language usage in the Jewish homeland, see
recently Walter Ameling, "Epigraphy and the Greek Language in Hellenistic
Palestine," *Scripta Classica Israelica* 34 (2015): 1–18, which includes references to
earlier publications; and Randall Buth and R. Steven Notley, eds., *The Language
Environment of First Century Judaea* (Leiden: Brill, 2014).

pagan deities as part of the routine of the Greek school.[7] For every sphere of life in the Roman world was marked with gods, and so marked with acknowledging them in one way or another.

But, in general, for these same Jews the "red-line" issue was cultic worship, that is, the direct participation in sacrifices to and worship of pagan gods. Conscientious Jews might have made all sorts of other moves in negotiating their lives, especially in diaspora cities, but by all accounts they typically avoided direct involvement in *cultus* to pagan deities.[8] That practice they termed "idolatry," the gravest of errors, and the fundamental sin from which all others proceeded.[9]

In making the worship of pagan deities the key boundary marker not to be crossed, ancient Jews in their own distinctive way affirmed the wider notion that worship was the key expression of religion in the ancient world. Both Jews and non-Jews agreed on this. So, for example, non-Jews tended to view Jewish refusal to join in worshipping the various deities of the Roman world as bizarre, offensive, antisocial, and even atheistic. For, as noted already, worship was how you affirmed the reality and validity of a deity; and so refusing to worship a deity (or deities) was effectively a denial of its (or their) reality and/or validity.

Moreover, in order to appreciate the significance of early Jesus-devotion, it is also important to note that the cultic

---

7. We might think of an analogy of sorts in the requirement formerly in many US states (now, so far as I know, dropped) that school days must open with students reciting the Lord's Prayer. Brave dissenters could ask to be excused, but I suspect that others simply stood and pretended to say the prayer to avoid the opprobrium of others. In the ancient Roman setting, Jews such as Philo may well have taken a similar course of action.

8. See, e.g., Peder Borgen, "'Yes,' 'No,' 'How Far?': The Participation of Jews and Christians in Pagan Cults," in *Paul in His Hellenistic Context*, ed. Troels Engberg-Pedersen (Minneapolis: Fortress, 1995), 30–59.

9. Note, e.g., the extended critique of idolatry in Wisdom of Solomon 13-15, which includes the notion that idolatry was the font of other sins (14:12).

exclusivity of ancient Jewish tradition extended beyond refusing
to worship the deities of other nations. In particular, it appears
that Jews also avoided worshipping the various heavenly beings
whom they saw as forming God's entourage, the vast and serried
ranks of angels and archangels. That is, ancient Jews refused
to worship foreign deities and the "home team" (so to speak)
as well. As I showed a few decades ago, this refusal extended to
principal angels and related heavenly beings (such as Michael),
exalted biblical heroes (such as Moses or Enoch), and even the
personifications of God's own attributes (such as Lady Wisdom
or God's Logos).[10] None of these figures was a separate object
of worship. There was no altar or sacrifice or worship ritual
devoted to any of them. I must underscore this point, as it has
been obscured in some recent publications that claim incor-
rectly that Jews included such beings in their worship practice.[11]

---

10. Larry W. Hurtado, *One God, One Lord: Early Christian Devotion and Ancient
Jewish Monotheism* (Philadelphia: Fortress, 1988; 2nd ed., Edinburgh: T&T Clark,
1998; 3rd ed., London: Bloomsbury T&T Clark, 2015).

11. E.g., recently Bart D. Ehrman, *How Jesus Became God: The Exaltation of a
Jewish Preacher from Galilee* (New York: HarperOne, 2014), 54–55, 61. Contra his
claim, however, we do not have evidence of Jews who worshipped "other divine
beings, such as the great angels." Cf. my analysis of relevant evidence regard-
ing high angels in *One God, One Lord*, 24–36. Ehrman cites Loren Stuckenbruck,
Angel Veneration and Christology (Tübingen: J.C.B. Mohr [Paul Siebeck], 1995), in
support of his claim. But Stuckenbruck distinguished between what he called
"veneration" of angels (essentially the conceptual prominence of angels in the
religious outlook of ancient Jews) and "cultic worship" (50n4), which he confirmed was firmly reserved for God alone, acknowledging the lack of evidence
of "angel veneration as a practice" within any Jewish religious group (103). The
specific "venerative" practices for which he found some evidence included occa-
sional invocations of angels (often with God) for assistance in desperate situa-
tions, a view of angels as exemplary for human worship of God (as, e.g., reflected
in the Qumran text Songs of the Sabbath Sacrifice), and verbal expressions
of thanks "in response to various functions or activities attributed to angels"
(200–201). He judged none of these, however, to amount to "cultic devotion"
to angels. But he suggested that what he called "venerative language," i.e., the
august descriptions of angels and descriptions of the functions of particular
high angels, may have helped to prepare earliest Jewish Christians to take the

In some cases, this or that figure is referred to in language that suggests some kind of divine status or quasi-deification, as illustrated in a Qumran text (11QMelchizedek) that in a striking move posits a mysterious figure named Melchizedek as the divine figure, *elohim*, of Psalm 82:1, who takes a prominent place among the heavenly "council of God" and exercises judgment.[12] The Hebrew of this verse is usually translated roughly as follows:

God [*elohim*] has taken his place [or "stands forth"] in the divine council [*ba'adat-el*]; in the midst of the gods [*elohim*] he holds judgment.

The Septuagint (LXX Psalm 81:1) shows an effort to make sense of the statement with its several references to divine beings:

God [*ho theos*] stands forth in the assembly of gods [*synagogē theōn*]; and in their midst he will judge gods [*theous diakrinei*].

It appears that this Qumran text reflects a distinctive move in identifying this Melchizedek figure as the *elohim* of Psalm 82:1 who stands up/stands forth in the heavenly council. This figure does not compete with God, however, but is apparently

---

further step of including Jesus programmatically in their cultic practice. Perhaps. But there is no actual evidence for this, no evidence that early Jesus followers pointed to or drew on the Jewish treatment of angels in justifying or expressing their devotion to Jesus in cultic practices. See my review of Stuckenbruck's book in *Journal of Theological Studies* 47 (1996): 248–53.

12. 11QMelchizedek (11Q13) 2.9–13. Text and translation in Florentino García Martínez and Eibert J. C. Tigchelaar, *The Dead Sea Scrolls: Study Edition* (Grand Rapids: Eerdmans; Leiden: Brill, 1997), 2:1206–9.

God's appointed head over the heavenly council of "gods" (who may include the angels of God's entourage and/or the various deities of the pagan nations). In the Qumran text, Melchizedek is thus effectively God's field marshal or vizier who is to lead in the eschatological battle against the forces of evil. To be sure, referring to this figure as the *elohim* of Psalm 82:1 is remarkable. But I emphasize again that, despite this kind of striking exegetical move, neither this Melchizedek nor any of the other various "chief agent" figures portrayed in various ancient Jewish texts were treated as a rightful recipient of cultic devotion. They, and the angels more broadly, might be referred to as "gods," but they were distinguished from the biblical deity precisely when it came to worship. I emphasize that Jews protected the uniqueness of their deity foremost by reserving cultic worship to him alone. Not only sacrifice, but prayer and adoration as well were typically directed to the one God.[13]

As an example of the evidence for my statement, consider the book of Tobit. On the one hand, the narrative features a high angel, Raphael, who (feigning to be a human) guides the young Tobias to his relatives in Media, ensures safety for Tobias and his bride, Sarah, and then guides the happy couple back home to Tobias's aged father, Tobit. Toward the end of the story, Raphael discloses his true nature and status as "one of the seven holy angels who present the prayers of the saints and enter into the presence of the glory of the Holy One" (Tobit 12:15). On the other hand, all of the numerous prayers in this book are directed solely to God.[14] Indeed, Raphael exhorts Tobit and Tobias to praise God and pray to God alone (12:6–7), and after

---

13. Again, I refer readers to my analysis of these matters in *One God, One Lord*, passim.

14. Prayers occupy a considerable place in Tobit: 3:1–6, 11–15; 8:5–9, 15–17; 11:1–2, 14–15; 13:1–18.

Raphael's revelation of his high angelic status, he urges them again to "give thanks to God," which they then do (12:20–22). Indeed, what follows is a lengthy prayer of praise by Tobit that is directed solely to God, with no mention of Raphael or any other figure (13:1–18). My point is that, even in this and other ancient Jewish texts that feature this or that principal angel centrally, often described in lofty terms, the prayers and worship are directed to the one God alone.[15]

This shows, by the way, that the interest in these various figures did not arise from a Jewish sense of distance or alienation from their God. When they prayed, they prayed directly to God, not to these figures. The evidence of Jewish prayer from the Greco-Roman period reflects a confidence that their God is near and hears. The "chief agent" figures were not substitutes for God but, instead, seem to have served as the expressions or vehicles of God's sovereignty, and as part of the depiction of God as like a great monarch with powerful figures in his service. So to reiterate the point again for emphasis, the dominant ancient Jewish stance on worship was not simply an antiforeigner attitude. Instead, there seems to have been a genuine concern to make the one God the sole legitimate recipient of worship, by which I mean in particular individual prayer and worship offered openly, and also corporate worship that functioned as the overt expression of Jewish religious identity.

---

15. See, e.g., Norman B. Johnson, *Prayer in the Apocrypha and Pseudepigrapha: A Study of the Jewish Concept of God*, SBLMS 2 (Philadelphia: Society of Biblical Literature, 1948); James H. Charlesworth, "Jewish Hymns, Odes, and Prayers (ca. 167 B.C.E.–135 C.E.)," in *Early Judaism and Its Modern Interpreters*, ed. Robert A. Kraft and G. W. E. Nickelsburg (Atlanta: Scholars Press, 1986), 411–36.; Tessel M. Jonquiere, *Prayer in Josephus*, AJEC 70 (Leiden: Brill, 2007); Michael Matlock, *Discovering the Traditions of Prose Prayers in Early Jewish Literature*, LSTS 81 (London: T&T Clark, 2012).

There is certainly evidence that some Jews engaged in "magical" practices that included the invocation of this or that powerful spirit, sometimes angelic beings.[16] But, of course, by definition "magic" involves secretive ritual acts that do not function as the corporate and identifying rituals of any given group. You engage in magic "by the dark of the moon," so to speak, not as an open expression of your religious affiliation and loyalty. The question is not what kinds of surreptitious rituals that some ancient Jews may have indulged in secretly, but instead what constituted the open/public worship pattern that ancient Jews professed and followed collectively. Moreover, as Gideon Bohak observed, the specifics of ancient Jewish magical practices actually indicate a distinction between God and the various other beings that could be invoked for this or that magical aim. Bohak concluded that the Jews who engaged in magical practices intended no competition or conflict with their exclusivity of worship to the one God.[17]

This exclusivity applied especially to worship/sacrifice in the Jerusalem temple of the Roman period, of course, and it is highly significant that no other figure was reverenced there, for this was the national shrine, the most blatant institutional expression of Jewish religion. There was no altar or sacrifice to any other figure than the one biblical deity.[18] Also, so far as we can tell, this exclusivity also included other Jewish religious settings such as synagogue gatherings. In ancient synagogues,

---

16. See, e.g., Peter Schäfer, "Magic and Religion in Ancient Judaism," in *Envisioning Magic: A Princeton Seminar and Symposium*, ed. Peter Schäfer and Hans G. Kippenberg (Leiden: Brill, 1997), 19–44; and now especially Gideon Bohak, *Ancient Jewish Magic: A History* (Cambridge: Cambridge University Press, 2008).

17. Bohak, *Ancient Jewish Magic*, 51–62, "Magic and Monotheism."

18. This exclusivity appears to distinguish the Jerusalem temple of the Hellenistic/Roman periods from the "preexilic" period.

it appears that any prayers or other ritual actions were directed solely to the one God. Even such a Jewish sectarian group as the Qumran community observed this strict limitation of worship to God alone.[19] The Qumran group sharply differentiated itself from the larger body of Jews in several matters, but shared in this firm cultic exclusivity.

But might the mysterious figure described in such august terms in the Similitudes of 1 Enoch be an exception? He is referred to in the text most frequently as "the Chosen/Elect One," but also as "the Righteous One," "that/this son of man" and "Messiah."[20] He is said to have been chosen before creation (38:2-3, 6-7). He will be revealed in the eschatological time and will preside over the destruction of the godless rulers of the earth (52:6-9), and he will even judge "Azazel" (the name given in the text to the satanic leader of evil forces) and his evil angels (55:4; 61:8-9). The Chosen One will sit on a glorious throne (45:3; 61:8),

19. The Qumran text Songs of the Sabbath Sacrifice was used to chant hymns *along with* angels (in heaven), but the songs were certainly not sung *to* angels. On this text, see James H. Charlesworth and Carol A. Newsom, eds., *Angelic Liturgy: Songs of the Sabbath Sacrifice* (Louisville: Westminster John Knox Press, 1999); Philip S. Alexander, *The Mystical Texts: Songs of the Sabbath Sacrifice and Related Manuscripts* (London: T&T Clark, 2006). On Qumran prayer practices, see Daniel K. Falk, *Daily, Sabbath, and Festival Prayers in the Dead Sea Scrolls* (Leiden: Brill, 1998), and on Qumran worship practice more broadly, Moshe Weinfeld, "Prayer and Liturgical Practice in the Qumran Sect," in *The Dead Sea Scrolls: Forty Years of Research*, ed. Devorah Dimant and Uriel Rappaport (Leiden: Brill, 1992), 241-57. On the relation of Qumran beliefs and practices to early Christian phenomena, L. W. Hurtado, "Monotheism, Principal Angels, and the Background of Christology," in *The Oxford Handbook of the Dead Sea Scrolls*, ed. Timothy H. Lim and John J. Collins (Oxford: Oxford University Press, 2010), 546-64.

20. The "Similitudes/Parables" of 1 Enoch = chaps. 37-71. This material is extant solely in the Ethiopic version of 1 Enoch. I draw here on the translation by George W. E. Nickelsburg and James C. VanderKam, *1 Enoch: The Hermeneia Translation* (Minneapolis: Fortress, 2012). For a recent study of the messianic figure in question, see Darrell D. Hannah, "The Elect Son of Man of the *Parables of Enoch*," in *"Who Is This Son of Man?" The Latest Scholarship on a Puzzling Expression of the Historical Jesus*, ed. Larry W. Hurtado and Paul L. Owen (London: T&T Clark, 2011), 130-58.

and all earth's inhabitants will fall down before him and "glorify and praise and sing hymns to the name of the Lord of Spirits [the way God is typically referred to in this text]" (48:4-5), and all kings and rulers will petition this Chosen One for mercy (62:9).

I want to make two cautionary observations about this figure, however. First, it is not clear that any passage in the Similitudes actually depicts the Chosen One as the recipient of corporate worship by God's elect/righteous.[21] Certainly, as noted already, the pagan kings and rulers offer him obeisance and beg him to show mercy, just as the conquered typically responded to their conquerors in the ancient world, but this is not really worship by a body of devotees. Part of the problem plaguing scholarly claims about these passages is a failure to understand that "worship" translates terms in various ancient languages (e.g., the Greek term *proskyneō*) that strictly designate the gesture of prostration before someone, whether a deity or a conqueror, or merely a social superior. Context is crucial in determining what specific kind of reverence is shown in the gesture, and in the case of 1 Enoch 62:9 what we have is simply a gesture of submission by conquered rulers. By contrast, it seems to me that where 1 Enoch depicts actual "cultic" worship as we would mean the term, that is, corporate praise and adoration by the redeemed

---

21. Cf., e.g., Ehrman, *How Jesus Became God,* 64–67, who erroneously claims otherwise. James A. Waddell, *The Messiah: A Comparative Study of the Enochic Son of Man and the Pauline Kyrios* (London: T&T Clark, 2011), exhibits the somewhat confused approach that also plagues some other studies. He fails to grasp that the exalted descriptions of the Chosen One do not constitute evidence that he was, or was to be, actually worshipped by the elect. As I showed in *One God, One Lord,* ancient Jews were quite ready to accord various "chief agent" figures exalted titles, and could refer to them in grand terms, but did not proceed to the cultic worship of these figures.

directed to a recipient in a setting that connotes reverence for a deity, it is directed to God alone (e.g., 61:6–11).[22]

Second, even those who nevertheless prefer to read the obeisance given to the Chosen One as cultic worship have to grant that there is no evidence that the Similitudes reflect the actual worship practices of any circle(s) of Roman-era Jews. At most, that is, the Similitudes depict in visionary mode events that may be *projected to take place in the future* when the predestined Chosen One is revealed. That is, we have visions of eschatological developments, but not reflections or evidence of the actual cultic practices of any Second Temple Jewish group, not even among those who wrote and read the Similitudes.[23] By contrast (as we will see), the New Testament writings reflect the actual devotional practices of identifiable circles of the early Jesus movement. These devotional practices constitute, therefore, a real and noteworthy historical development in the ancient Jewish context in which they first appeared.

I therefore contend that even the depiction of the august Chosen One of the Similitudes does not really give us an exception to the pattern of cultic exclusivity characteristic of

---

22. Cf., e.g., 1 En. 48:4–7, which predicts that all earth's inhabitants will "fall down and worship before him" (v. 5, the Chosen One). This makes appearance of the Chosen One the *occasion* and *setting* for the reverence; but it is not clear that the worship is directed to him. For the text adds that the peoples "will glorify and bless and sing hymns to the name of the Lord of Spirits," which suggests that the worship is actually directed to God, not the Chosen One.

23. Aramaic fragments of 1 Enoch were found among the Qumran texts, but none comes from the portion now referred to as the "Similitudes" or "Parables" of Enoch (chaps. 37–71). See J. T. Milik, ed., *The Books of Enoch: Aramaic Fragments of Qumran Cave 4* (Oxford: Clarendon, 1976). So, it remains unclear exactly when these chapters were composed and when or how they made their way into the composite work now known as 1 Enoch. But there is now an increasing tendency to posit a date of the composition of the Similitudes in the (early?) first century CE. See, e.g., the discussion of date and provenance in the Introduction to Nickelsburg and VanderKam, *1 Enoch*.

Roman-era Jewish tradition. In some earlier scholarship the pro-
liferation of various "chief agent" figures (such as the Chosen
One of 1 Enoch) was taken as compromising the uniqueness of
God, but the evidence actually indicates the opposite. As noted
previously, evidence of Jewish prayer practice, for example,
indicates that prayer was typically addressed directly to God,
and to God alone.[24] The various chief agent figures that appear
in Second Temple Jewish texts do not indicate a weakening of
the Jewish sense of relationship to their God, or any blurring of
God's uniqueness. Instead, each of these figures serves to picture God in august terms, like a great emperor with a vizier to
serve as chief servant of divine purposes, and with a vast host of
other servants as divine entourage. But when it came to prayer
and worship, Jews typically went straight to God. The various
chief agent figures were often described impressively, but they
were in no sense a rival to, or confused with, God.[25]

Moreover, it actually appears that Jewish cultic exclusivity
may have become more emphatic by the Roman period than
it had been in some earlier centuries.[26] The Maccabean crisis,
which is portrayed in Jewish texts as resistance to the Seleucid
attempt to assimilate the Jews religiously, seems to have resulted
in a greater concern thereafter to maintain Jewish religious

24. I cite my discussion of the data in *One God, One Lord*, 17–40.

25. Note Philo of Alexandria's distinction between the "satraps" of a "Great
King" and the honors due to the king himself: "in the same way anyone who
pays the same tribute to the creatures as to their Maker may be assured that he
is the most senseless and unjust of men" (*Decal.* 61 [Colson, LCL]).

26. Hurtado, "Ancient Jewish Monotheism," 386–91. In the "preexilic" period,
and perhaps on into the Persian period as well, Israelite religion seems to have
been considerably more open to multiple deities. See, e.g., Mark S. Smith, *The
Early History of God* (San Francisco: Harper & Row, 1990). The papyri from the
Jewish colony at Elephantine may preserve something of this earlier pattern.
See, e.g., Alejandro F. Botta, "Elephantine, Elephantine Papyri," in *The Eerdmans
Dictionary of Early Judaism*, ed. John J. Collins and Daniel C. Harlow (Grand
Rapids: Eerdmans, 2010), 574–77.

distinctiveness, and this above all in worship.[27] One further implication that is particularly relevant here is that in that period it was more unlikely that pagan notions of apotheosis or practices such as the emperor cult could have been influential in the origins of Jesus-devotion.[28]

27. This is my argument in the article cited earlier, "Ancient Jewish Monotheism."

28. For my critique of recent proposals about the supposed influence of ruler cults on the origin of Jesus-devotion, see the new epilogue in the third edition of *One God, One Lord*, 143–49.

CHAPTER 4

THE EARLY CHRISTIAN "MUTATION"

In the context of ancient Jewish "chief agent" traditions and the cultic exclusivity characteristic of Jewish devotion, the place of Jesus in earliest Christian belief and, particularly, in devotional practice takes on a remarkable, striking historical significance. From my 1988 book, *One God, One Lord*, onward in various publications I have referred to the novel "mutation" in Jewish devotional practice reflected in our earliest Christian texts.[1] By the term "mutation" I mean a development that has both recognizable connections with the "parent" religious tradition (in this case, ancient Judaism) and also identifiably new features that distinguish the development from its parent tradition. I have also characterized the early Christian development

---

1. Larry W. Hurtado, *One God, One Lord: Early Christian Devotion and Ancient Jewish Monotheism* (Philadelphia: Fortress Press; London: SCM, 1988; 2nd ed., Edinburgh: T&T Clark, 1998; 3rd ed., London: Bloomsbury T&T Clark, 2015), chap. 5, "The Early Christian Mutation."

as constituting a "dyadic" devotional pattern in which the risen/
exalted Jesus featured centrally and uniquely with God as virtu-
ally a co-recipient of cultic devotion.[2] In the following discussion
I survey this distinctive development, echoing and summarizing
my analysis offered in previous publications.

I emphasize the particular historical significance of the place
of Jesus in early Christian devotional practice. To be sure, however, the christological claims and rhetoric reflected in New
Testament writings are noteworthy and well known. So I trust
that it will be sufficient simply to cite some of the relevant texts
by way of illustration. Already in our earliest extant evidence
(Letters of Paul, from ca. 50-60 CE), Jesus is regularly referred
to as "Christ" (Messiah), the unique Son of God, and the *Kyrios*
to whom believers are to be obedient, to invoke and reverence
as the Lord of the gathered worship circle.[3] Also, in the earliest
years, Old Testament texts that originally referred to God were

---

2. In some of my earlier publications, I referred to a "binitarian" devotional
pattern, e.g., *Lord Jesus Christ: Devotion to Jesus in Earliest Christianity* (Grand
Rapids: Eerdmans, 2003), 134-53. But, because this term was sometimes mis-
construed as importing into first-century Christian practices the "ontological"
categories of Christian theological discussions of the third century and later
(despite my efforts to make clear how I intended the term), I now use the term
"dyadic." Whichever term I have used simply describes the early Christian devotional pattern in which both God and Jesus are uniquely linked as recipients.

3. Werner Kramer, *Christ, Lord, Son of God*, SBT 50 (Naperville: Allenson,
1966), is a classic discussion of these key christological titles, but he puts
his foot wrong on some things, especially in his claim that for Paul Jesus'
divine sonship was not important. Nothing could be further from the truth!
Cf. Larry W. Hurtado, "Son of God," in *Dictionary of Paul and His Letters*, ed.
Gerald F. Hawthorne, Ralph P. Martin, and Daniel G. Reid (Downers Grove, IL:
InterVarsity Press, 1993), 900-906; Hurtado, "Jesus' Divine Sonship in Paul's
Epistle to the Romans," in *Romans and the People of God*, ed. Sven K. Soderlund
and N. T. Wright (Grand Rapids: Eerdmans, 1999), 217-33; and especially Martin
Hengel, *The Son of God: The Origin of Christology and the History of Jewish-Hellenistic
Religion* (Philadelphia: Fortress, 1976). On Paul's use of *Christos* (Christ), see now
Matthew V. Novenson, *Christ among the Messiahs: Christ Language in Paul and
Messiah Language in Ancient Judaism* (New York: Oxford University Press, 2012),
who shows persuasively that, contrary to much previous opinion, the term

applied to Jesus (somewhat similarly to the application of Psalm 82:1 to the Melchizedek figure noted earlier, but on a far wider scale).[4] Probably the most striking example of this use of Old Testament texts is the appropriation of the statement in Joel 2:32, "all who call upon the name of the LORD [*Yahweh*] shall be delivered," making Jesus the "Lord" who is to be "called upon" for salvation, as in Romans 10:9–13 (a passage that I will return to later in this discussion).

As another example of the high claims about Jesus that characterize New Testament discourse, in his future parousia, Jesus is the one in whom the eschatological manifestation of God's prophesied return in triumph and glory will be fulfilled, as in 1 Thessalonians 4:13–5:11.[5] In this passage, Jesus is "the Lord" who will descend in great glory to gather the redeemed to himself (4:17), and the Old Testament prophetic hope of "the day of the LORD" is to be fulfilled in "the Lord Jesus Christ" (5:1–9), through whom salvation will be granted.

Also, in addition to Jesus' eschatological role, Paul even refers to Jesus as the preexistent and unique "one Lord" through whom all things were created (1 Cor 8:4–6), in what looks to many scholars like a distinctive and "dyadic" adaptation of the traditional Jewish confession of God's uniqueness, the Shema:

---

carries a messianic connotation, and in Paul's beliefs Jesus' messianic status remained important.

4. David B. Capes, *Old Testament Yahweh Texts in Paul's Christology*, WUNT 2/47 (Tübingen: J. C. B. Mohr [Paul Siebeck], 1992).

5. Larry J. Kreitzer, *Jesus and God in Paul's Eschatology*, JSNTSup 19 (Sheffield: JSOT Press, 1987); and my corrective to N. T. Wright on this matter: Larry W. Hurtado, "YHWH's Return to Zion: A New Catalyst for Earliest High Christology?," in *God and the Faithfulness of Paul*, ed. Christoph Heilig, J. Thomas Hewitt, and Michael F. Bird (Tübingen: Mohr Siebeck, 2016), 417–38.

> Although there may be so-called gods in heaven or
> on earth—as indeed there are many "gods" and many
> "lords"—yet for us there is one God, the Father, from
> whom are all things and for whom we exist, and one Lord,
> Jesus Christ, through whom are all things and through
> whom we exist.

Note that the exclusivity of the "one God" is extended here
and matched to the "one Lord, Jesus Christ," the assertion of
God's uniqueness extended to reflect a similar claim about Jesus.
In a comparatively more extended christological text (Phil 2:6–
11), Paul depicts Jesus famously as having been "in the form of
God [*en morphē theou*]" prior to his taking on "the form of a slave"
and "being born in human likeness" and making himself obedient even to the point of crucifixion (vv. 6–8).[6] Paul then writes
that the risen/exalted Jesus has been given "the name above
every name" and is to receive universal acclamation (vv. 9–11):

> so that at the name of Jesus every knee should bow, in
> heaven and on earth and under the earth, and every
> tongue confess that Jesus Christ is Lord, to the glory of
> God the Father.

Remarkably, this statement reflects a quite obvious appropriation of Isaiah 45:23, which is part of one of the most emphatic

---

6. There is a slight ambiguity in the Greek phrasing, *en morphē theou* (v. 6),
which could equal "in the form of God" or "in the form of a god," this phrase
intended to contrast with *morphēn doulou* (v. 7). Among the huge number of
studies of Phil 2:6–11, I immodestly point to my own in my book, *How on Earth
Did Jesus Become a God? Historical Questions about Earliest Devotion to Jesus* (Grand
Rapids: Eerdmans, 2005), 83–107. See also the multiauthor volume, Ralph Martin
and Brian Dodd, eds., *Where Christology Began: Essays on Philippians 2* (Louisville:
Westminster John Knox, 1998).

declarations of God's uniqueness in the entire biblical canon. But in Philippians 2:9–11 this Old Testament text is apparently interpreted and adapted to declare that eschatological obeisance is rightly to be given to the exalted Jesus, this in turn to redound to the glory of God the Father. That is, the eschatological supremacy of God prophesied in Isaiah 45:23 is to be fulfilled in the universal obeisance to be given to the exalted Jesus.

In another and still more extended passage (2 Cor 3:12–4:6), Paul laments the veiled hearts and hardened minds of fellow Jews who do not share his faith in Christ, and declares that when one "turns to the Lord" (3:14–16) one is than able to perceive "the glory of the Lord" (3:18), and in this text quite obviously the Lord is Jesus.[7] Then Paul refers to "the glory of Christ, who is the image [eikōn] of God" (4:4), and he climactically celebrates God's bestowal of "the light of the knowledge of the glory of God in the face of Christ" (4:6). Similarly to the scenario in Philippians 2:9–11 depicting the universal submission to be given to Jesus, in another text, 1 Corinthians 15:20–28, Paul refers to Jesus seated "at the right hand" of God as the divine plenipotentiary to whom everything is to be made subservient. To cite another text, in Romans 8:34, Paul also refers to Jesus "at the right hand" of God, where he intercedes for believers.[8]

I endorse Martin Hengel's memorable statement cited earlier about the christological development reflected in these and other passages that must be placed within about eighteen years at most, the time elapsed between Jesus' crucifixion and

---

7. On this remarkable body of text, see now the in-depth analysis by Michael Cover, *Lifting the Veil: 2 Corinthians 3:7–18 in Light of Jewish Homiletic and Commentary Traditions*, BZNW 210 (Berlin: De Gruyter, 2015).

8. On the topos of the exalted Jesus as God's "right hand" and its historical context, see especially Martin Hengel, "'Sit at My Right Hand!': The Enthronement of Christ at the Right Hand of God and Psalm 110:1," in *Studies*

the earliest letters of Paul. This chronological perspective is important if we are to appreciate the enormity of what was involved in the eruption of christological claims in the early Jesus movement.

Indeed, building on Hengel's chronological observations, I have contended that the most crucial christological development likely took place within the very few years (perhaps as little as one year) between Jesus' execution and Paul's Damascus road experience (which is commonly dated ca. 30–35 CE). For Paul's brief references to that experience, especially his characterization of it as God's revelation to him of Jesus as God's Son (Gal 1:15–16), indicate that the cognitive content of this experience was profoundly christological. Essentially, Paul came to see Jesus in a wholly different light, no longer as a justifiably executed false teacher (which was likely his view prior to his revelatory experience), but as the uniquely approved Son of God.[9] It is plausible that Paul's contrast noted earlier between a hardened and veiled inability to recognize Jesus' glorious status and the transformation that comes "when a man turns to the Lord" (2 Cor 3:12–4:6) reflects Paul's own experience. Certainly, Paul seems to have turned abruptly and quickly from attempting to destroy the young Jesus movement to an enthusiastic and committed allegiance to Jesus.

---

in *Early Christology* (Edinburgh: T&T Clark, 1995), 119–225. The image seems to most scholars to be drawn from Ps 110:1, where God invites another figure to sit at his "right." See, e.g., David M. Hay, *Glory at the Right Hand: Psalm 110 in Early Christianity* (Nashville: Abingdon, 1973). In a recent essay, however, I have also pointed to Ps 16 as an influence: "Early Christological Interpretation of the Messianic Psalms," *Salmanticensis* 64 (2017): 73–100. Now republished in Larry W. Hurtado, *Ancient Jewish Monotheism and Early Christian Jesus-Devotion: The Context and Character of Christological Faith* (Waco: Baylor University Press, 2017), 559–82.

9. Max Wilcox, "'Upon the Tree'—Deut 21:22–23 in the New Testament," *Journal of Biblical Literature* 96 (1977): 85–99.

Moreover, I take it that the revelation of Jesus' high significance likely meant that Paul capitulated to the sort of christological claims that he had previously found offensive and
that had helped to provoke his previous efforts to "destroy" the
young Jesus movement.[10] To be sure, Paul claimed a distinctive
divine calling to carry out his mission to gentiles, but he never
claimed any distinctiveness in his core christological beliefs or
in the devotional practices reflected in his letters.[11] Instead, the
impression he gives in his letters (e.g., 1 Cor 15:1-7) is that he
and the Jerusalem church of fellow Jewish believers were essentially one in these matters.[12] Paul was unhesitating in expressing
sharp disagreement and displeasure with those whom he saw
as impeding his gentile mission and who demanded that gentiles should convert to full Torah observance, as reflected in the
Letter to the Galatians as well as other texts. But he never indicated that he and they differed over christological beliefs, and
that is a most eloquent silence.

But, in addition to these remarkably early christological
developments to which Paul gave assent, that is, beliefs about
Jesus' significance, I contend that the place of Jesus in earliest
Christian devotional practice is, in historical terms, still more
astonishing. I repeat that, when viewed in the light of the Jewish
concerns to restrict worship to the one God alone, the programmatic place of Jesus in earliest Christian devotion amounts to a

---

10. I have supported this claim in my essay, "Pre-70 CE Jewish Opposition
to Christ-Devotion," *Journal of Theological Studies* 50 (1999): 50–57 (35–58), this
essay republished in my book, *How on Earth Did Jesus Become a God?*, 152–78. In
addition to Gal 1:15-16, with others, I take 2 Cor 3:4–4:6 as also reflecting Paul's
own experience of revelation about Jesus' glorious significance. On this passage, see, e.g., Carey C. Newman, *Paul's Glory-Christology: Tradition and Rhetoric*,
NovTSup 69 (Leiden: Brill, 1992), 229–35.

11. See my discussion of "Early Pauline Christianity" in my book, *Lord Jesus
Christ*, 79–153.

12. I have discussed Judean Jewish Christianity in *Lord Jesus Christ*, 155–216.

novel and historically significant "mutation." And I am not alone in this judgment. For example, a century ago, Johannes Weiss referred to the early emergence of the cultic reverence of the risen Jesus as "the most significant step of all in the history of the origins of Christianity."[13]

As discussed earlier here, in his influential book *Kyrios Christos*, Wilhelm Bousset took roughly a similar view about the historical significance of this development.[14] But, unlike Weiss, Bousset asserted that the cultic reverence of Jesus reflected in Paul could not have emerged in "the primitive Palestinian community." Instead, he insisted that it was the *Hellenistic* community (by which Bousset meant what he called "the Gentile Christian Primitive Community") in which this development so important for the history of religions took place. Bousset granted that this development happened early, indeed, so early that it characterized the form of Christian faith and practice into which Paul was introduced after his Damascus road experience. But, I repeat, Bousset contended that the central place of the risen Jesus in the worship practices of circles of believers—"this particular doubling of the object of veneration in worship"—was inconceivable in an authentic Jewish setting, and could only have developed in diaspora locations such as Antioch, where pagan religious influences were stronger and, he contended, constituted the decisive factor.

Along with earlier scholars such as Weiss and Hengel, however, for over a quarter of a century I have argued that the

---

13. Johannes Weiss, *Das Urchristentum* (Göttingen: Vandenhoeck & Ruprecht, 1917). I cite the English translation, *The History of Primitive Christianity*, 2 vols. (London: Macmillan, 1937; republished as *Earliest Christianity* [New York: Harper & Brothers, 1959]), 1:37.

14. Wilhelm Bousset, *Kyrios Christos: A History of Belief in Christ from the Beginnings of Christianity to Irenaeus*, trans. John E. Steely (Waco, TX: Baylor University Press, 2013), 136, 147.

evidence points strongly to the origin of the cultic veneration of Jesus as lying in thoroughly Jewish circles of the Jesus movement such as the Jerusalem church.[15] From recent observations by various other scholars, it appears that this argument has helped to generate a growing groundswell of support, and is now perhaps the dominant view among scholars who have worked on the question in recent years.[16]

In conclusion, I emphasize two key points. First, the cultic veneration of the risen Jesus presumed already as typical of Jewish and gentile circles of the Jesus movement in Paul's Letters originated remarkably early. Second, originating in Jewish circles of believers, it constituted a novel and remarkable "mutation" in the devotional pattern otherwise characteristic of Roman-era Jewish tradition. Indeed, I contend that in historical terms the eruption of this cultic veneration of Jesus is perhaps the most significant development in emergent early Christianity, particularly in the first century.[17]

---

15. E.g., my discussion in *One God, One Lord*, 2–5; and a more extensive discussion in my later book *Lord Jesus Christ*, 155–216. Much earlier, I noted several major problems in Bousset's portrayal of earliest devotion to Jesus in my essay "New Testament Christology: A Critique of Bousset's Influence," *Theological Studies* 40 (1979): 306–17.

16. E.g., Andrew Chester, "High Christology When, When and Why?," *Early Christianity* 2 (2011): 22–50, esp. 38–39; Richard Bauckham, "Devotion to Jesus Christ in Earliest Christianity: An Appraisal and Discussion of the Work of Larry Hurtado," in *Mark, Manuscripts, and Monotheism: Essays in Honor of Larry W. Hurtado*, ed. Chris Keith and Dieter T. Roth (London: Bloomsbury T&T Clark, 2014), 176–200, esp. 176; and Ehrman, *How Jesus Became God*, 235.

17. The only development of possibly rival significance is Paul's gentile mission and the programmatically trans-ethnic spread of the Jesus movement.

CHAPTER 5

JESUS IN EARLIEST CHRISTIAN DEVOTIONAL PRACTICE

So what specific phenomena constituted this cultic venera-tion of Jesus, and how significant were they? New Testament scholars have tended to focus almost entirely on the christolog-ical terms and beliefs expressed in New Testament texts, but I contend that the place of Jesus in early Christian worship prac-tice is even more remarkable in its cultural context. Before I address this question further, it is important to observe that the prominent place of the risen Jesus in early Christian devotion as reflected in the Pauline Letters and some other early texts did not typically involve any displacement or replacement of God.[1] Jesus was not reverenced at God's expense, so to speak. Nor was Jesus reverenced as a second god. Instead, what we

---

1. Contra the claim by Arthur Cushman McGiffert, *The God of the Early Christians* (Edinburgh: T&T Clark, 1924), that Jesus became the god of early Christians, especially among converted pagans.

dominantly see from our earliest texts onward is a distinctive "dyadic" devotional pattern, in which Jesus is included along with God as recipient, and Jesus' divine status is articulated with reference to God.[2] As I shall note, typically in early Christian texts, worship and prayer were directed to God, either simply or through Jesus and/or in Jesus' name. Even when Jesus is the explicit recipient of cultic devotion, it seems typically to have been intended as responding to God's exaltation of Jesus, and so as constituting also worship of God. Nevertheless, in its historical context, particularly the noted ancient Jewish concern to avoid compromising God's uniqueness by including any other figure as a recipient of worship, the place of Jesus in earliest Christian devotional practice is remarkable.

In publications stretching over a number of years, with a concern to make the discussion as precise as possible, I have tried to focus scholarly attention on specific practices that constitute the "dyadic" devotional pattern reflected in our earliest Christian texts. So in the present discussion I shall be brief.[3] I underscore the point, made in the previous chapter, that in particulars and even more in their collective force, these phenomena constitute a novel and noteworthy "mutation" in Jewish devotional practice. I also insist that any discussion about the place of Jesus in earliest Christian worship should address these phenomena.[4]

---

2. Larry W. Hurtado, *God in New Testament Theology* (Nashville: Abingdon, 2010), esp. 49-71.

3. See, e.g., my discussion in *Lord Jesus Christ: Devotion to Jesus in Earliest Christianity* (Grand Rapids: Eerdmans, 2003), 138-51.

4. One of the shortcomings of J. D. G. Dunn's study *Did the First Christians Worship Jesus? The New Testament Evidence* (Louisville: Westminster John Knox, 2010), is his failure to engage the full range of the devotional practices that I have laid out. See my review: *Journal of Theological Studies* 61 (2010): 736-40.

Because Paul's Letters afford us our earliest Christian texts and evidence, I shall make particularly frequent reference to them. But I emphasize also that Paul's acquaintance with the beliefs and practices of the young Jesus movement was both early and wide. His own initiation into faith in Jesus was within the very earliest years (or months) after Jesus' execution, and his personal contacts included believers in Jerusalem and Judea, Damascus, Antioch, and the various cities where he then established churches. So, unless there is good reason not to do so, we are entitled to take Paul's evidence as widely representative of the early Christian movement.

PRAYER

Typically, as noted, in early Christian texts, prayer is offered to God "the Father," but God is also typically (or at least often) linked with Jesus and/or identified implicitly or explicitly with reference to Jesus: for example, as "the God and Father of our Lord Jesus Christ" (2 Cor 1:3-4).[5] In Romans 1:8 Paul refers to giving thanks to God "through Jesus Christ," which at the least reflects his view of Jesus' place in prayer, and may allude to the real practice of invoking Jesus in making prayers to God. Various

---

5. Other instances of similar phrasing in Col 1:3; Eph 1:3, 17. Joseph Jungmann, *The Place of Christ in Liturgical Prayer*, trans. A. Peeler, 2nd ed. (London: Geoffrey Chapman, 1965), argued that early liturgical prayer (typically in the Eucharist) was to God through Christ: "It was not until the end of the fourth century that we meet, by way of exception, prayers to Christ the Lord, and these are not within the Eucharistic celebration proper but in the fore-Mass and in Baptism" (164). But he granted that private prayer directly to Christ is attested from Paul onward, and that it particularly characterized the prayers of martyrs, and he judged that it was more attested in apocryphal texts (165-69). Cf., however, Boris A. Paschke, "Tertullian on Liturgical Prayer to Christ: New Insights from *De Spect.* 25.5 and *Apol.* 2.6," *Vigiliae Christianae* 65 (2011): 1-10, who argues that liturgical prayer to Christ was practiced more often than Jungmann judged. See also Richard Bauckham, "The Worship of Jesus," in his book *The Climax of the Covenant: Studies on the Book of Revelation* (Edinburgh: T&T Clark, 1993), 118-49.

so-called prayer-wish statements in Paul's Letters likely reflect
actual prayer practice also, in which God and Jesus are addressed
and invoked together, as in 1 Thessalonians 3:11–13:

> Now may our God and Father himself, and our Lord Jesus,
> direct our way to you; and may the Lord [Jesus the refer-
> ent here] make you increase and abound in love to one
> another and to all, as we do to you.

There are similar examples of this in 2 Thessalonians 2:16–
17, where Jesus and God are invoked jointly (in this case, Jesus
mentioned first), and in 2 Thessalonians 3:5, where "the Lord"
appealed to is certainly Jesus, as must also be the case in 2
Thessalonians 3:16, "Now may the Lord of peace himself give
you peace at all times in all ways. The Lord be with you all."

In the curious passage in 2 Corinthians 12:1–10, where Paul
refers to his heavenly ascent (one of his many "visions and revelations," 12:1), he says that he repeatedly appealed to "the Lord"
(who here is Jesus) to remove the "thorn in the flesh" that Satan
was allowed to inflict on him (12:8–9). This is clearly an example of direct prayer specifically to Christ. Similarly, Acts 9:10–19
relates a vision of "the Lord" (Jesus) in which Ananias is directed
to go to welcome Saul/Paul, and Ananias engages in a kind of
prayer-conversation with Christ about the matter.

Paul's "grace and peace" salutations at the beginning of his
letters likewise typically invoke God and Jesus together (e.g., 1
Cor 1:3; 2 Cor 1:2) as the joint sources of the blessings, as in this
example in 1 Corinthians 1:3: "Grace to you and peace from God
our Father and the Lord Jesus Christ" (similarly, Rom 1:7; 2 Cor
1:2; Gal 1:3; Phil 1:2). The equally typical "grace benedictions" that
conclude Paul's letters feature Jesus even more prominently, as
in 1 Corinthians 16:23: "The grace of the Lord Jesus be with you,"

and similarly in Romans 16:20; Galatians 6:18; Philippians 4:23; 1 Thessalonians 5:28; 2 Thessalonians 3:18; Philemon 25.[6] These salutations and benedictions are widely thought to represent Paul's use of early Christian liturgical formulas, and so are to be taken as reflective of a corporate devotional practice that involved appeals to and invocation of the exalted Jesus.[7]

To characterize the evidence of the place of Jesus in early Christian prayer practice more broadly, Jesus is posited in various early Christian texts as the unique intercessor/advocate before God on behalf of the elect, as the teacher and role model of prayer, as the recipient of prayer (as we have noticed, with God or alone), and as the efficacious basis of Christian prayer.[8] Note, for example, Paul's encouragement to believers that no one can condemn them in God's sight, for Christ is "at the right hand of God" and there "intercedes for us" (Rom 8:34). Collectively, these ideas and practices are unprecedented and unparalleled, especially the evidence of direct appeals to Jesus in the corporate worship setting, and they gave early Christian prayer a distinctive character marked and shaped by the exalted Jesus.

---

6. The sonorous and well-known triadic formula in 2 Cor 13:14, "The grace of the Lord Jesus Christ and the love of God and the fellowship of the Holy Spirit be with you all," is unique, but still reflects the central place of Jesus in these liturgical-sounding expressions.

7. See, e.g., Peter T. O'Brien, "Benediction, Blessing, Doxology, Thanksgiving," in *Dictionary of Paul and His Letters,* ed. Gerald F. Hawthorne, Ralph P. Martin, and Daniel G. Reid (Downers Grove, IL: InterVarsity Press, 1993), 68–71 (with further bibliography).

8. Texts and discussion given in Larry W. Hurtado, "The Place of Jesus in Earliest Christian Prayer and Its Import for Early Christian Identity," in *Early Christian Prayer and Identity Formation,* ed. Reidar Hvalvik and Karl Olav Sandnes (Tübingen: Mohr Siebeck, 2014), 35–56; republished in my collection of essays, *Ancient Jewish Monotheism and Jesus-Devotion: The Context and Character of Early Christological Faith* (Waco, TX: Baylor University Press, 2017), 615–34.

INVOCATION/CONFESSION

I turn now to a closely related devotional practice. In 1 Corinthians 1:2, Paul refers to believers simply as "all those who in every place call on the name of our Lord Jesus Christ," which likely reflects the common practice of invoking Jesus in the worship setting.[9] It is remarkable that Paul refers to this practice as in itself an adequate designation of believers. The practice both unifies believers in a shared devotional practice and distinguishes them thereby as well. Similarly, note the characterization of those whom the young and zealous Saul sought out to arrest as "all who call upon" Jesus' name (Acts 9:14, 21).

Paul also refers to this practice in Romans 10:9-13, using the same verb (*epikaleō*), which here and in other instances (including a number in the OT) is used to designate the ritual invocation of a deity.[10] The striking thing in this passage in Romans is that Paul appropriates this expression from the Old Testament (Joel 2:32; in the Hebrew text 3:5), which originally designated invocation of Yahweh, to refer here to the ritual invocation of Jesus: "Everyone who calls upon the name of the Lord will be saved" (Rom 10:13). It is a bold move to appropriate this Old Testament text to make Jesus the referent. But it is even more remarkable that this ritual invocation of Jesus was obviously such a central part of earliest Christian devotional/worship practice. For this invocation of Jesus seems to have been a key component of the corporate worship gathering, both in the churches that Paul

---

9. So, e.g., Hans Conzelmann, *1 Corinthians: A Commentary on the First Epistle to the Corinthians*, Hermeneia (Philadelphia: Fortress, 1976), 23; and the more extended discussion in Anthony C. Thiselton, *The First Epistle to the Corinthians: A Commentary on the Greek Text*, NIGTC (Grand Rapids: Eerdmans, 2000), 78-80.

10. OT instances include Gen 13:4; 26:25; 1 Kgs 18:24-26; Ps 116:4. See, e.g., W. Kirchschläger, "ἐπικαλέω," in *Exegetical Dictionary of the New Testament*, ed. Horst Balz and Gerhard Schneider (Grand Rapids: Eerdmans, 1990-93), 2:28-29.

founded and, so he claims in 1 Corinthians 1:2, more universally in early Christian circles.

In confirmation of this, Paul's well-known use of the Aramaic liturgical phrase *marana tha* in 1 Corinthians 16:22 must reflect a similar cultic invocation of Jesus in Aramaic-speaking circles of believers as well as in Paul's Greek-speaking churches composed largely of gentiles.[11] This little phrase is well-recognized as telltale evidence that a cultic devotion to Jesus goes back to the earliest times and circles of the Jesus movement.[12] Paul's use of this Aramaic formula in this letter to Greek-speaking, and largely (or entirely) gentile believers in Corinth, and without bothering to translate it, must surely show that they were already acquainted with it. Indeed, it is likely that Paul had conveyed this liturgical formula to the Corinthian church in the course of his initial missionary work there, likely with the intention of promoting thereby a sense of linkage with the devotional practices of Aramaic-speaking believers in Roman Judea. This aim is also probably reflected in Paul's use of the Aramaic term *Abba* for God (Gal 4:6; Rom 8:15), this term also used in contexts that reflect prayer and worship practices. Note that these two linguistic links to Aramaic-speaking circles of believers refer respectively to Jesus (the *Mar* invoked in *Maranatha*) and

11. See my discussion in *One God, One Lord*, 106–7; and *Lord Jesus Christ*, 140–41; and also the extended review of scholarly analysis in Thiselton, *1 Corinthians*, 1348–52; and Anders Eriksson, *Traditions as Rhetorical Proof: Pauline Argumentation in 1 Corinthians*, Coniectanea Biblica, New Testament Series 29 (Stockholm: Almqvist & Wiksell, 1998), 279–98. The expression appears also in Didache 10:6 in the eucharistic prayer there, but, as reflected in what seems the Greek equivalent in Rev 22:20, "Come, Lord Jesus!," it is likely that *maranatha* originally (or additionally) was an appeal for Jesus's parousia.

12. Martin Hengel, "Abba, Maranatha, Hosanna und die Anfänge der Christologie," in *Studien zur Christologie, Kleine Schriften IV* (Tübingen: Mohr Siebeck, 2006), 496–534. A. E. J. Rawlinson memorably referred to *marana tha* as "the Achilles' heel of the theory of Bousset": *The New Testament Doctrine of the Christ* (London: Longmans, Green, 1926), 235.

to God (the *Abba*, to whom also believers appeal), an interesting reflection of what I have termed the "dyadic" pattern of earliest Christian devotional practice.

In addition to the invocation of Jesus, it appears that a ritual (probably collective) "confession" of Jesus' exalted status was characteristic of early Christian worship. For Romans 10:9–13 also includes a reference to this practice: "If you confess [*homologeō*] with your lips that Jesus is Lord, and believe in your heart that God raised him from the dead, you will be saved." There is another probable allusion to this practice in 1 Corinthians 12:3, which ascribes the confession "Jesus is Lord" to the impulse of the Holy Spirit. This confession marked the gathered circle, and also prefigured the universal future acclamation that Paul posits in Philippians 2:9–11, "Jesus Christ is Lord." That is, the ritual confession of Jesus in the gathered church represented a ritual anticipation and assertion of that future universal acclamation, the corporate worship of the churches thus having a certain eschatological tenor.

BAPTISM

The characteristic initiation rite practiced in early Christian circles was baptism, and our earliest evidence indicates that the rite included the invocation of Jesus by name (e.g., Acts 2:38; 8:16; 10:48; 22:16). The phrasing, baptism "in/into Jesus' name" suggests that the meaning was that the baptized person thereby became marked as the property of Jesus or at least that the baptism was specifically identified with reference to Jesus.[13] By all indications, baptism in/into Jesus' name arose initially in

---

13. Lars Hartman, *"Into the Name of the Lord Jesus": Baptism in the Early Church* (Edinburgh: T&T Clark, 1997); and now the wide-ranging study by Everett Ferguson, *Baptism in the Early Church: History, Theology, and Liturgy in the First Five Centuries* (Grand Rapids: Eerdmans, 2009).

Jewish circles of the Jesus movement in Roman Judea, making this linkage of the initiation rite with a figure other than God both remarkable and unparalleled in Roman-era Jewish tradition. No other figure occupied a similarly central place in any other Jewish group of the time.

John the Baptizer was certainly noted for his promotion of baptism as a ritual of repentance. But there is no indication that this ritual involved any appeal to him, either during his own ministry or among his followers after his death. To cite another example, despite the importance of the Teacher of Righteousness for the Qumran community, there is no evidence that he was invoked in worship or as part of their initiation ritual. Paul's curious statement that the ancient Israelites who fled Egypt were "all baptized into Moses in the cloud and in the sea" forms part of Paul's treatment of the events in the exodus narrative in 1 Corinthians 10:1-5 as foreshadowing instructively the situation of believers. In effect, Paul retrojects into the exodus narrative a significance and character derived from the ritual practice of early Christian circles, imaginatively making the flight through the sea and the presence of the cloud that followed Israel a "baptism." There is no evidence, however, that actual Jewish immersion practices included the invocation of Moses or any other figure. So baptism "in/into" the name of Jesus, involving the explicit invocation of him, is another distinctive feature of the "dyadic" devotional pattern of early Christianity.

THE LORD'S SUPPER

Granting that there may well have been a certain variety of early Christian common-meal practices, it is nevertheless highly likely that a meal signifying the religious meaning of the group featured widely in Christian circles from the earliest years onward.[14] Again, Paul's Letters give us our earliest references to a shared meal as part of the church gathering. It is important to note that Paul claims to have been given a tradition about this meal "from the Lord" (1 Cor 11:17–34), which likely means that he received it from predecessors in Christian faith.[15] In this tradition, the meal is closely tied to Jesus' death as "for you" and establishing a "new covenant" (11:23–25). That is, the meal is to be a "remembrance" of Jesus (*anamnēsis*, 11:25) in which believers declare "the Lord's death" (*ton thanaton tou kyriou katangellete*, 11:26), which surely marks this meal distinctively as deriving its meaning specifically from Jesus. It is "the Lord's supper" (*kyriakon deipnon*, 11:20), and therefore believers must take part in an appropriate manner, or risk "profaning the body and blood of the Lord" (11:27), and consequent "judgment" upon themselves (11:29).

In another passage in 1 Corinthians (10:14–22), in some ways more striking still, Paul compares and contrasts this Christian meal with the cult meals dedicated to pagan deities. He refers to the Christian meal as "the Lord's supper," which involves partaking of "the cup of the Lord" and "the table of the Lord" (1 Cor 10:21). In the context, these terms give the meal an overtly sacral character. "The table of the Lord" here is directly contrasted with "the table of demons," that is, the altars of the pagan deities and the eating of sacrificial offerings to them. Paul's strictures about avoiding the worship of pagan gods (e.g., 10:14) surely reflect his inherited Jewish concern to protect God's uniqueness. But,

---

14. Paul F. Bradshaw, *Eucharistic Origins* (London: SPCK, 2004); Jerome Kodell, *The Eucharist in the New Testament* (Wilmington, DE: Michael Glazier, 1988). Dennis E. Smith, *From Symposium to Eucharist: The Banquet in the Early Christian World* (Minneapolis: Fortress, 2003), emphasizes the place of shared meals in various social groups of the Roman era.

15. See Thiselton, *1 Corinthians*, 866–68, for discussion and engagement with other publications.

to underscore the point, in the immediate context, the "Lord" whose table believers are to hold to exclusively is obviously Jesus. The cultic exclusivity characteristic of Second Temple Jewish practice is modified ("mutated") to include Jesus as the "Lord" of the gathered church, an equivalent exclusivity accorded to his "table." This central place of Jesus in the common meal of early Christian circles, and the cultic significance accorded to "the Lord's supper" in which he is so central, make this rite yet another unparalleled phenomenon that is expressive of the uniquely dyadic shape of early Christian devotion.[16]

HYMNS, PSALMS, AND SPIRITUAL SONGS

It is commonly granted that "hymns" (in the generic sense of the word), namely, sung/chanted praise compositions, formed a characteristic feature of early Christian worship.[17] Paul refers to a "psalm" as one of the phenomena of the worship gathering (1 Cor 14:26), and Colossians 3:16-17 urges believers to sing (corporately it seems) "psalms, hymns, and spiritual songs" (also Eph

---

16. Cf., e.g., K. G. Kuhn, "The Lord's Supper and the Communal Meal at Qumran," in *The Scrolls and the New Testament*, ed. Krister Stendahl (London: SCM, 1958; repr., New York: Crossroad, 1992), 65-93, esp. 77-78.

17. The scholarly literature is now considerable, as reflected in the references given in *Lord Jesus Christ*, 147n161. See, e.g., Martin Hengel, "The Song about Christ in Earliest Worship," in *Studies in Early Christology* (Edinburgh: T&T Clark, 1995), 227-91; Leonard L. Thompson, "Hymns in Early Christian Worship," *Anglican Theological Review* 55 (1973): 458-72; Reinhard Deichgräber, *Gotteshymnus und Christushymnus in der frühen Christenheit: Untersuchungen zu Form, Sprache und Stil der frühchristlichen Hymnen*, SUNT 5 (Göttingen: Vandenhoeck & Ruprecht, 1967). Joseph Kroll, *Die christliche Hymnodik bis zu Klemens von Alexandreia* (Königsberg: Hartungsche Buchdruckerei, 1921), remains a valuable survey of the first two centuries. Michael Lattke, *Hymnus: Materialien zu einer Geschichte der antiken Hymnologie*, NTOA 19 (Göttingen: Vandenhoeck & Ruprecht; Fribourg: Editions universitaires, 1991), surveys the use of hymns in ancient religion more broadly.

5:18–20).[18] The "psalms" mentioned in these texts may refer to the liturgical chanting of Old Testament Psalms or possibly to new compositions expressing praise to God and Christ.[19] It is thus not entirely clear whether "psalms, hymns, and spiritual songs" all designate roughly the same thing or three distinguishable types of compositions.[20] In Colossians 3:16, the more likely variant reading has the singing done "to God," whereas in the parallel phrasing in Ephesians 5:19 it is "to the Lord" (probably to be taken as Jesus).[21] It is relevant, however, to note that the New Testament texts often identified as possibly derived from early hymns (e.g., Phil 2:6–11; Col 1:15–20; John 1:1–18; Eph 5:14; 1 Tim 3:16) and other early texts that are explicitly labeled as worship songs (e.g., Rev 4:11; 5:9–10, 12–13; 7:12; 11:17–18; 15:3–4) are all heavily concerned with celebrating Jesus and his redemptive work.[22]

---

18. I take the plural forms of the exhortations in Col 3:16–17 as reflecting activities associated with the church gathered.

19. E.g., Horst Balz, "ψαλμός," in Balz and Schneider, *Exegetical Dictionary*, 3:495–96.

20. This uncertainty seems to have been there for ancient readers too, as may be reflected in the textual variants in Col 3:16, with a good many witnesses (e.g., C³ D¹ and the mass of medieval manuscripts) having "psalms and hymns and spiritual songs" (which suggests three somewhat distinguishable types of musical compositions), and others (e.g., 𝔓46 א B D*) having "psalms, hymns, spiritual songs" (which may suggest that the words were taken as three designations of the same sort of composition). Of course, it is also likely that the first reading is a harmonization with the wording in Eph 5:19.

21. Again, the variant reading "to the Lord" in Col 3:16 in some manuscripts is probably a harmonization with Eph 5:19.

22. There is also, of course, Pliny's frequently cited report that in their gatherings the Christians sang "to Christ as to a god" (*Epistles* 10.96.7). Phil 2:6–11 continues to generate scholarly debate as to whether it really is, or derives from, an early christological hymn. See, e.g., Gordon D. Fee, "Philippians 2:5–11: Hymn or Exalted Pauline Prose?," *Bulletin for Biblical Research* 2 (1992): 29–46; Joseph A. Marchal, "Expecting a Hymn, Encountering an Argument: Introducing the Rhetoric of Philippians and Pauline Interpretation," *Interpretation* 61 (2007): 245–55; Ralph Brucker, *"Christushymnen" oder "epideiktische Passagen"? Studien zum Stilwechsel im Neuen Testament und seiner Umwelt* (Göttingen: Vandenhoeck & Ruprecht, 1997); Michael Peppard, "'Poetry,' 'Hymns' and 'Traditional Material'

But, whether sung to the risen Jesus or sung to God about Jesus, these references to, and examples of, early Christian hymns/odes reflect the prominent place of Jesus in the gathered worship of early Christian circles, and constitute another devotional practice that, again, has no parallel in the Jewish tradition. For we have no reference to odes/chants celebrating any other figure having a similar centrality in the worship gatherings of other Second Temple Jewish groups. This is a further reflection of the "mutation" characteristic of earliest Christian devotional practice.

PROPHECY

Prophetic oracles were another feature of early Christian worship gatherings (e.g., 1 Cor 12:10; Rom 12:6).[23] These oracles were often spoken and received by believers as inspired by God's Spirit, but in at least some instances were also offered as inspired by, and/or the words of, the risen Jesus. Acts 13:1–3 depicts a worship scene where the Holy Spirit speaks, which must mean via a prophetic oracle, ordering that Barnabas and Paul be "set apart for me ... for the work to which I have called them." Though ascribed to the Spirit, the first-person voice of the oracle must be the risen Jesus, who is depicted earlier in Acts as calling Paul for an international mission (Acts 9:15–17).

---

in New Testament Epistles or How to Do Things with Indentations," *Journal for the Study of the New Testament* 30 (2008): 319–42; Jennifer R. Strawbridge and Benjamin Edsall, "The Songs We Used to Sing? Hymn 'Traditions' and Reception in Pauline Letters," *Journal for the Study of the New Testament* 37 (2015): 290–311; Michael Wade Martin and Bryan A. Nash, "Philippians 2:6–11 as Subversive *Hymnos*: A Study in the Light of Ancient Rhetorical Theory," *Journal of Theological Studies* 66 (2015): 90–138; and the multiauthor volume, Clemens Leonhard and Hermut Löhr, eds., *Literature or Liturgy? Early Christian Hymns and Prayers in Their Literary and Liturgical Context in Antiquity* (Tübingen: Mohr Siebeck, 2014); see now also Matthew E. Gordley, *New Testament Christological Hymns* (Downers Grove, IL: InterVarsity Press, 2018).

23. See esp. David E. Aune, *Prophecy in Early Christianity and the Ancient Mediterranean World* (Grand Rapids: Eerdmans, 1983).

Whatever the judgment of scholars today about the historicity of this particular scene in Acts 13, the author obviously expected the ancient Christian readers to recognize the sort of phenomenon recounted. So it is at least indirectly a witness to the beliefs and experiences of first-century Christian circles.

But the most obvious and well-known example of prophecy delivered as the words of the risen Jesus is surely the book of Revelation. The work opens with a vision of the glorified Jesus (described in 1:9–16) and John is then ordered to "Write what you see," which is followed by a set of oracles to the seven churches in Revelation 2–3. In each of these the glorified Christ speaks words of warning and encouragement via the author. Yet these oracles are also "what the Spirit says to the churches" (2:7, 11, 17, 29; 3:6, 13, 22). Prophetic oracles seem to have been a familiar feature of earliest Christian worship, and these oracles were apparently often spoken as the words of God, the Holy Spirit, and/or Christ, interchangeably. It is not clear that there was much effort to differentiate or discriminate in the matter.

This is confirmed in 1 Corinthians 12:4–11, where Paul lists various charismatic phenomena that include several types of inspired/prophetic speech, and in a triadic manner he ascribes them all to "the same Spirit," "the same Lord" (who here must be Jesus), and "the same God" (12:4–6). In light of the negative attitude in Old Testament texts against prophecy of any source than the one God, and the lack of parallels of oracles in other early Jewish groups in the name of any figure other than God, the phenomenon of prophecy ascribed to the risen Jesus is extraordinary.[24] It surely puts the risen Jesus in a role rather directly comparable to God's, and this in the corporate worship setting.

---

24. Note, e.g., the warning against prophets who speak in the name of some deity other than Yahweh in Deut 13:1–11.

CHAPTER 6

CONCLUSION

These several phenomena quickly surveyed here form a constellation of devotional practices that is distinctive in the Roman-era setting, and particularly in the context of the Jewish tradition that was the matrix in which these practices first emerged. Over against the wider Roman-era religious environment with its many and varied deities, the earliest Christian texts reflect the cultic exclusivity (which I have termed "ancient Jewish monotheism") inherited from the Second Temple Jewish context in which the Jesus movement arose, initially as a distinctive variant form within that Second Temple Jewish tradition. But what made the Jesus movement distinctive in its devotional practice was its dyadic shape, involving the inclusion of the risen Jesus as a recipient along with the one God. As noted earlier, although it first emerged in this ancient Jewish context, this dyadic devotional pattern was, by all extant evidence, distinctive, apparently unique to the Jesus movement. We have no evidence of any other Jewish group of the time in which any figure other than the one God was given the kinds of devotion that are attested in our earliest Christian texts.

In my view, this early and rapid "mutation" in typical Jewish devotional practice could have occurred only if earliest participants felt themselves obliged to take part. That is, I think that they must have come to the conviction that God required them to reverence Jesus, and so the dyadic pattern that emerged was, in their eyes, actually obedience to the one God. For them, it was not a departure from faithfulness to the one God, but instead the devotional response that this God now required as the appropriate response to his exaltation of Jesus and designation of him as the Lord to whom all were now to give obeisance.

In previous publications I have proposed that this conviction arose via powerful religious experiences that struck recipients with the force of revelations.[1] I suggest that these experiences included visions of the exalted/glorified Jesus such as we see reflected in texts such as the resurrection narratives, the vision ascribed to Stephen in Acts 7:55-56, and the vision portrayed in such detail in Revelation 1:9-16, which conveyed to recipients the confirmation that Jesus had been exalted and glorified by God. Further, I suggest that there were prophetic oracles that expressed Jesus' exaltation and God's will that he be reverenced. In addition, we must allow for the effects of a "charismatic exegesis" of Old Testament texts that suddenly seemed to testify to Jesus. For example, this last phenomenon must lie behind the novel appropriation of Isaiah 45:22-23 in Philippians 2:9-11 that I noted earlier.

---

1. Larry W. Hurtado, "Religious Experience and Religious Innovation in the New Testament," *Journal of Religion* 80 (2000): 183-205; Hurtado, "Revelatory Experiences and Religious Innovation in Earliest Christianity," *Expository Times* 125 (2014): 469-82.

In any case, it is clear that at a remarkably early point circles of Jewish believers came to the strong conviction that God had exalted Jesus to unique heavenly glory and now required him to be reverenced in their worship. This conviction is directly expressed in John 5:22–23, which declares that it is God's will "that all should honor the Son just as they honor the Father. Whoever does not honor the Son does not honor the Father who sent him." But it is unlikely that this conviction emerged at the time of the composition of the Gospel of John. Instead, we have here a concise and somewhat polemical expression of the matter set here in the context of challenge from Jewish critics of Jesus' validity.[2] But, as I noted earlier, it seems likely that there was opposition to the reverence given to Jesus in circles of Jewish believers from the earliest years and from fellow Jews such as the young Pharisee Saul of Tarsus.

Curiously, as I lamented at the outset of this discussion, in scholarly studies of early belief in Jesus the character and characteristics of early Christian worship are still an often overlooked or underestimated body of evidence. But, to reiterate the point for emphasis (an emphasis much needed!), in the historical context of the early Roman period in which worship was the central expression of religion, and in light of evident Jewish sensitivity about worship, the inclusion of Jesus as recipient of cultic devotion in early Jewish-Christian circles represents an extraordinary development. In historical terms, even more clearly than the much-studied christological rhetoric and

---

2. With most scholars, I take this and other passages in the Gospel of John as reflecting the situation of believers in the "post-Easter" period. The distinctive character of the Gospel of John is that the narrative of Jesus' ministry is rendered in light of the situation and issues of believers in the post-Easter decades, which included pronounced Jewish opposition, reflected in the distinctively Johannine references to believers being expelled from "the synagogue" (e.g., John 9:22; 12:42; 16:2–4).

claims, the cultic reverence given to Jesus signals that the risen Jesus quickly acquired a divine status comparable and uniquely related to the one God. This seems to have happened so rapidly that it is already presumed in our earliest texts, and was initially a novel "mutation" in circles in the Roman-era Jewish tradition. These same early Christian texts also give no indication that it was a matter of difference or disputation among the varied circles that made up the early Jesus movement. There may have been some initial reluctance from some, but to judge from our evidence (especially the Letters of Paul) this Jesus-devotion characterized both Pauline and other streams of early Christianity, Jewish as well as gentile congregations of the time.

I repeat: The programmatic inclusion of the exalted Jesus with God in the corporate cultic devotional practice of earliest circles in the Jesus movement certainly constituted a novel, apparently unique, "dyadic" devotional pattern. Although the theological consequences of this occupied Christians in the following centuries, the decisive step in treating Jesus as sharing in some way in divine glory and status was taken remarkably early, and was expressed both in christological rhetoric and, most importantly, distinctively, and remarkably in this dyadic devotional pattern.

LORD AND GOD

Through his words and actions, Jesus of Nazareth excited expectations that he was (or would be) the Messiah.[1] That Jesus inspired this hope likely led the Roman authorities to crucify him. Jesus didn't actually claim divinity for himself, and he wasn't worshipped as such during his earthly ministry. The ascription of divine status to Jesus and the accompanying devotional practices that are reflected in the New Testament arose only after—though astonishingly soon after—Jesus' crucifixion. Key to this development were experiences ("visions") of the resurrected Jesus, which generated in the earliest circles of Jewish believers the conviction that God had raised Jesus (bodily) from death and exalted him to a unique heavenly status and glory.

---

1. Reproduced with permission. Copyright © 2014 by *The Christian Century*. "Lord and God" by Larry W. Hurtado is reprinted by permission from the July 21, 2014, issue of *The Christian Century*.

Further developments in christological belief over the ensuing decades and centuries led to the classic doctrine of the Trinity.

That, in a nutshell, is the thrust of Bart Ehrman's book [*How Jesus Became God: The Exaltation of a Jewish Preacher from Galilee*[2]]. To anyone familiar with a historical approach to the topic, these will not be novel conclusions. Indeed, they have been affirmed by a significant number of New Testament scholars, especially over the past several decades. That an astonishing "high Christology" erupted quite soon after Jesus' crucifixion, and that the risen Jesus featured remarkably in the corporate devotional practices of earliest believers, has been increasingly recognized. As the great German New Testament scholar Martin Hengel observed about developments in the 20 years between Jesus' execution and the earliest letters of Paul, "in essentials more happened in Christology within these few years than in the whole subsequent seven hundred years of church history."

However, Ehrman's book is intended for readers generally unacquainted with this scholarly work. Among those readers he obviously aims to have a dramatic impact. Many Christians unacquainted with the historical data will assume that beliefs about Jesus' divine status derive from Jesus' own claims, and many non-Christians will likewise assume that the validity of traditional Christian beliefs about Jesus depends upon whether Jesus actually made corresponding claims. For both kinds of readers, the "news" that Jesus didn't actually make the sort of claims for himself that earliest believers made about him may seem somewhat sensational.

As in his other popular books, Ehrman clearly seeks not simply to inform but also to stir controversy among this varied

---

2. Bart D. Ehrman, *How Jesus Became God: The Exaltation of a Jewish Preacher from Galilee* (New York: HarperOne, 2014).

readership. More specifically, he hopes to startle naive traditionalist Christians, nettle anxious apologists of Christian faith, and reassure fellow agnostics (Ehrman's self-description) and skeptics that there is justification for their doubt. (He is obviously able to stir a response: published almost simultaneously with this book is a multiauthor riposte, *How God Became Jesus: The Real Origins of Belief in Jesus' Divine Nature*, released by Zondervan.)

Ehrman's polemical agenda may well make for a lively discussion and a marketable book, but it also lessens somewhat his ability to give a balanced historical picture. Ehrman, who teaches at the University of North Carolina in Chapel Hill, gained prominence by way of a string of books with a similarly sensational tone aimed at a general readership on a variety of topics—variants in New Testament manuscripts (*Misquoting Jesus*), the problem of evil (*God's Problem*), and pseudonymous writings in the Bible (*Forged*). These books generated appearances on *The Daily Show* and *The Colbert Report* and phenomenal sales, at least compared to most books by scholars. In all these works he makes frequent reference to his own journey from naive and fundamentalist Christian to voluble (but generally genial) agnostic. Along with (and as another result of) his popular books, he often engages in public debates with Christian apologists, adding to his public stature.

In those prior books, Ehrman drew more directly on his own scholarly expertise. In this one he focuses on matters on which he himself has not been a noted contributor. He draws heavily (and respectfully) on the work of a number of other scholars (including my own work, such as *Lord Jesus Christ: Devotion to Jesus in Earliest Christianity*) who in recent decades have probed the origins of belief in Jesus as divine. Ehrman is often good at making scholarly arguments accessible. Unfortunately, in a few matters he oversimplifies or misconstrues things, and in other cases his claims and arguments appear one-sided.

An example of oversimplifying: in the first chapter Ehrman rightly notes that the Roman world was full of gods and deified humans (especially deified rulers), and he suggests that this phenomenon helps explain the emergence of beliefs about Jesus as divine. But he fails to indicate that for Roman-era Jews the plurality of deities and demigods and the practice of deifying rulers were repellent, even blasphemous. More of an explanation is needed as to how the multiplicity of deities in the Roman environment could have been a relevant and facilitating factor for considering Jesus divine in the circles of devout Jews among whom (as Ehrman readily grants) the divinity of Jesus was first asserted.

An example of his intrusive polemical concern is his discussion of what we can and cannot know about Jesus' resurrection. He points out that historians cannot answer the question of whether God actually raised Jesus from death and exalted him to heavenly glory. Historians can observe that early believers claimed to have seen the risen Jesus and can trace the effects of these claims, but as historians they cannot judge whether these claims are valid or not, for that is a theological or philosophical judgment. Ehrman professes to have no concern for either establishing or refuting these claims; he aims simply to trace their historical effects.

But he wanders from these strictures in a section where he likens early Christian experiences of the risen Jesus to such hallucinatory phenomena as "visions" of deceased loved ones. And such phenomena aren't true analogies. The grief experiences he cites don't typically involve a resurrected loved one in glorified form, who is exalted to heavenly glory at God's right hand. This fact suggests that something other than grief experiences was at work in the "visions" of the risen Jesus. Ehrman's discussion seems more intended to counter Christian apologists' references to resurrection appearances than to offer a balanced consideration. His earlier claim about sidestepping the question of the validity of early Christian claims seems coy.

Polemical concerns also intrude on his curiously prolonged argument that Jesus likely wasn't given a proper burial but was cast into a criminal's grave or left for carrion. His account seems designed more to challenge Christian claims about an empty tomb than to provide a balanced historical analysis of relevant burial practices. He does not cite examples of the ancient Jewish view that burial of the dead—including criminals and, notably, even those crucified—is a solemn religious duty (e.g., Tobit 1:16–18; Josephus, *Jewish War* 4.317). This Jewish concern is materially demonstrated in the only extant remains of a Roman-era crucified man, which were found properly entombed at Giv'at Ha-Mivtar (in Israel).

Another problem is Ehrman's discussion of Jesus' use of the expression "the Son of Man." He claims that Jesus (having either coined the expression or appropriated it from some unknown source) used the phrase to refer to a future figure, not himself. But if the expression wasn't a fixed and known title (as most scholars now recognize, and which Ehrman grants), how then would Jesus' disciples have grasped what he was talking about? It seems much more plausible that Jesus took the Hebrew/Aramaic idiom "son of man" and gave it a particularizing force, "*the* Son of Man," using it as his distinctive self-referential designation. This is also rather clearly how the idiom functions in the Gospels.

Curiously, Ehrman thinks that the early Christians thought the incarnation meant that Jesus was "temporarily human." On the contrary, in traditional Christian teaching Jesus' incarnation is an irrevocable assumption of human nature, and his resurrected body prefigures the glory to be accorded also to believers (e.g., Phil. 3:21).

Ehrman thinks it is highly significant that the New Testament writers don't identify Jesus as God the Father. It's true that they don't, but neither did the subsequent classical expressions of Christology, even expressions of Jesus' divinity "in a complete, full, and perfect sense" (Ehrman's phrase). Instead, from Justin Martyr onward the classic Christian writers emphasized that "the Father" and "the Son" were "numerically distinct."

In his discussion of the origins of beliefs about Jesus' divine status, Ehrman makes a point of distinguishing between "exaltation" Christology (Jesus' divine status is conferred by God at his resurrection) and "incarnation" Christology (Jesus is a "preexistent" divine being). To be sure, New Testament writings reflect these two emphases. One exaltation statement, Romans 1:3-4, refers to Jesus as "designated/declared the Son of God with power according to the Spirit of holiness through resurrection from the dead." As Ehrman explains helpfully, this text is one of a number in which Paul apparently incorporates confessional formulas that derive from a much earlier period and had already become traditional by the time he wrote his epistles (during the fifties of the first century).

Ehrman then opines that incarnation Christology came about "somewhat later," granting, however, that it was "remarkably early"—so early that it is already presupposed by Paul. He does not consider evidence from ancient Jewish sources (especially apocalyptic texts such as 1 Enoch) that the "preexistence" of eschatological figures was a Jewish theological trope. This evidence suggests that Jesus' preexistence could well have been an almost immediate corollary of the conviction that God had exalted him uniquely to heavenly/divine glory as the eschatological redeemer, the Messiah.

This, in turn, would explain why (as Ehrman also grants) these two types of christological statements are often combined in the earliest sources. Illustrative of this is the famous hymnic passage in Philippians 2:6-11, in which most scholars (including Ehrman) see the preexistent and divine Jesus described as first becoming "incarnate" as a man (vv. 6-8) and then subsequently exalted by God to a uniquely high status as "Kyrios," to be acknowledged by all spheres of creation (vv. 9-11). In short, it's not all that clear that first-generation Christians distinguished as sharply as Ehrman does between claims about Jesus' exaltation and his preexistence, or saw them as in tension with each other.

Ehrman's assertion that Paul saw Jesus as an angelic being is yet another curiosity. For Ehrman, this view is key to Paul's Christology. But Ehrman's discussion rests far too heavily on his claim (not shared by most interpreters) that in Galatians 4:14 Paul identifies Jesus as the/an "angel of God." Instead, Paul's statement that the Galatians had received him "as an angel of God, as Christ Jesus," seems to most exegetes to be an ascending set of alternatives. Ehrman also ignores evidence that Paul distinguished Jesus from the angels (e.g., Rom. 8:31-39). I would add that there is no evidence that angels (or any putative "Son of Man") received worship in the gatherings of any known Roman-era Jews. So the remarkable place of the risen Jesus in earliest Christian worship cannot be explained as a consequence of an alleged view of him as an angel.

In sum, this book elicits a mixed response. On the one hand, Ehrman is a generally good communicator, and the book may well introduce many readers to some of the issues and approaches involved in the scholarly investigation of Christian origins. But at points his argument is either somewhat misinformed or dubious.

The astonishing early Christian claims about the risen Jesus' divine status and the accompanying constellation of devotional practices appear to constitute a novel development in the Roman-era setting. They are in contrast to Jewish or "pagan" religious phenomena. These claims and practices are perhaps now so familiar both to Christians and non-Christians that their sheer novelty and astonishing character are no longer noticed. If Ehrman's book provokes further interest in the remarkable eruption of Jesus devotion in earliest Christianity, it will have had a good effect.

SCHOLARLY WORKS CITED

Alexander, Philip. *The Mystical Texts: Songs of the Sabbath Sacrifice and Related Manuscripts*. London: T&T Clark, 2006.

Althaus, Paul. "Unser Herr Jesus: Eine neutestamentliche Untersuchung: Zur Auseinandersetzung mit W. Bousset." *Neue Kirchliche Zeitschrift* 26 (1915): 439–57.

Ameling, Walter. "Epigraphy and the Greek Language in Hellenistic Palestine." *Scripta Classica Israelica* 34 (2015): 1–18.

Aune, David E. *Prophecy in Early Christianity and the Ancient Mediterranean World*. Grand Rapids: Eerdmans, 1983.

Balz, Horst. "ψαλμός." In Vol. 3 of *Exegetical Dictionary of the New Testament*, ed. Horst Balz and Gerhard Schneider, 495–96. Grand Rapids: Eerdmans, 1990–93.

Barclay, John M. G. *Jews in the Mediterranean Diaspora: From Alexander to Trajan (323 BCE–117 CE)*. Edinburgh: T&T Clark, 1996.

Bauckham, Richard. "Devotion to Jesus Christ in Earliest Christianity: An Appraisal and Discussion of the Work of Larry Hurtado." In *Mark, Manuscripts, and Monotheism: Essays in Honor of Larry W. Hurtado*, edited by Chris Keith and Dieter T. Roth, 176–200. London: Bloomsbury/T&T Clark, 2014.

———. "The Worship of Jesus in Apocalyptic Christianity." *New Testament Studies* 27 (1981): 322–41.

———. "The Worship of Jesus." In *The Climax of Prophecy: Studies on the Book of Revelation*, 118–49. Edinburgh: T&T Clark, 1993.

———. *God Crucified: Monotheism and Christology in the New Testament.* Carlisle, UK: Paternoster, 1998.

———. *Jesus and the God of Israel: God Crucified and Other Studies on the New Testament's Christology of Divine Identity.* Milton Keynes, UK: Paternoster, 2008.

Beard, Mary, John North, and Simon Price. *Religions of Rome.* Cambridge, UK: Cambridge University Press, 1998.

Boers, Hendrikus. "Jesus and Christian Faith: New Testament Christology since Bousset's Kyrios Christos." *Journal of Biblical Literature* 89 (1970): 450–56.

Bohak, Gideon. *Ancient Jewish Magic: A History.* Cambridge, UK: Cambridge University Press, 2008.

Borgen, Peder. "'Yes,' 'No,' 'How Far?' The Participation of Jews and Christians in Pagan Cults." In *Paul in His Hellenistic Context*, edited by Troels Engberg-Pederson, 30–59. Minneapolis: Fortress, 1995.

Botta, Alejandro F. "Elephantine, Elephantine Papyri." In *The Eerdmans Dictionary of Early Judaism*, edited by John J. Collins and Daniel C. Harlow, 574–77. Grand Rapids: Eerdmans, 2010.

Bousset, Wilhelm. *Kyrios Christos: A History of Belief in Christ from the Beginnings of Christianity to Irenaeus.* Translated by John E. Steely. Nashville: Abingdon Press, 1970. Reprint, Waco, TX: Baylor University Press, 2013. First published in German 1913, 1921 by Vandenhoeck & Ruprecht (Göttingen).

———. *Jesus der Herr: Nachträge und Auseinandersetzungen zu "Kyrios Christos."* FRLANT n.s. 8. Göttingen: Vandenhoeck & Ruprecht, 1916.

Bradshaw, Paul F. *Eucharistic Origins.* London: SPCK, 2004.

Bremmer, Jan N. "Atheism in Antiquity." In *The Cambridge Companion to Atheism*, edited by Michael Martin, 11–26. Cambridge, UK: Cambridge University Press, 2007.

Brodd, Jeffrey, and Jonathan L. Reed, eds. *Rome and Religion: A Cross-Disciplinary Dialogue on the Imperial Cult.* Atlanta: Society of Biblical Literature, 2011.

Brucker, Ralph. *"Christushymnen" oder "epideiktische Passagen"? Studien zum Stilwechsel im Neuen Tesetament und seiner Umwelt.* Göttingen: Vandenhoeck & Ruprecht, 1997.

Buth, Randall, and R. Steven Notley, eds. *The Language Environment of First Century Judaea.* Leiden: Brill, 2014.

Capes, David B. *Old Testament Yahweh Texts in Paul's Christology.* WUNT 2/47. Tübingen: J. C. B. Mohr [Paul Siebeck], 1992.

Casey, Maurice. *From Jewish Prophet to Gentile God: The Origins and Development of New Testament Christology.* Louisville: Westminster John Knox, 1991.

Chadwick, Henry. *Origen: Contra Celsum.* Cambridge, UK: Cambridge University Press, 1965.

Charlesworth, James H. "Jewish Hymns, Odes, and Prayers (ca. 167 B.C.E.-135 C.E.)." In *Early Judaism and Its Modern Interpreters,* edited by Robert A. Kraft and G. W. E. Nickelsburg, 411-26. Atlanta: Scholars Press, 1986.

Charlesworth, James H., and Carol A. Newsom, eds. *Angelic Liturgy: Songs of the Sabbath Sacrifice.* Louisville: Westminster John Knox Press, 1999.

Chester, Andrew. "High Christology When, When and Why?" *Early Christianity* 2 (2011): 22-50.

Conzelmann, Hans. *1 Corinthians: A Commentary on the First Epistle to the Corinthians.* Hermeneia. Philadelphia: Fortress, 1976.

Cover, Michael. *Lifting the Veil: 2 Corinthians 3:7-18 in Light of Jewish Homiletic and Commentary Traditions.* BZNW 210. Berlin: De Gruyter, 2015.

Davis, Carl J. *The Name and Way of the Lord.* JSNTSup 129. Sheffield: JSOT Press, 1996.

Deichgräber, Reinhard. *Gotteshymnus und Christushymnus in der frühen Christenheit: Untersuchungen zu Form, Sprache und Stil der frühchristlichen Hymnen.* SUNT 5. Göttingen: Vandenhoeck & Ruprecht, 1967.

Drachmann, Anders B. *Atheism in Pagan Antiquity.* London: Gyldendal, 1922.

Dunn, J. D. G. *Did the First Christians Worship Jesus? The New Testament Evidence.* Louisville: Westminster John Knox, 2010.

Ehrman, Bart D. *How Jesus Became God: The Exaltation of a Jewish Preacher From Galilee*. New York: HarperOne, 2014.

Eriksson, Anders. *Traditions as Rhetorical Proof: Pauline Argumentation in 1 Corinthians*. Coniectanea Biblica, New Testament Series 29. Stockholm: Almqvist & Wiksell, 1998.

Falk, Daniel K. *Daily, Sabbath, and Festival Prayers in the Dead Sea Scrolls*. Leiden: Brill, 1998.

Fee, Gordon D. "Philippians 2:5–11: Hymn or Exalted Pauline Prose?" *Bulletin for Biblical Research* 2 (1992): 29–46.

Ferguson, Everett. *Baptism in the Early Church: History, Theology, and Liturgy in the First Five Centuries*. Grand Rapids: Eerdmans, 2009.

Fletcher-Louis, Crispin H. T. "The Worship of Divine Humanity as God's Image and the Worship of Jesus." In *The Jewish Roots of Christological Monotheism: Papers From the St. Andrews Conference on the Historical Origins of the Worship of Jesus*, edited by Carey C. Newman, James R. Davila, and Gladys S. Lewis, 112–28. Leiden: Brill, 1999.

———. *Jesus Monotheism, Vol. 1, Christological Origins: The Emerging Consensus and Beyond*. Eugene, OR: Cascade, 2015.

Fredriksen, Paula. "Mandatory Retirement: Ideas in the Study of Christian Origins Whose Time Has Come to Go." *Studies in Religion/Sciences Religieuses* 35 (2006): 231–46. Reprinted in *Israel's God and Rebecca's Children: Christology and Community in Early Judaism and Christianity*, edited by David B. Capes, et al., 25–38. Waco, TX: Baylor University Press, 2007.

García Martínez, Florentino, and Eibert J. C. Tigchelaar. *The Dead Sea Scrolls: Study Edition*. Grand Rapids: Eerdmans; Leiden: Brill, 1997.

Gordley, Matthew E. *New Testament Christological Hymns*. Downers Grove, IL: InterVarsity Press, 2018.

Gruen, Erich S. *Diaspora: Jews Amidst Greeks and Romans*. Cambridge, MA: Harvard University Press, 2002.

Hannah, Darrell D. "The Elect Son of Man of the Parables of Enoch." In *"Who Is This Son of Man?" The Latest Scholarship on a Puzzling Expression of the Historical Jesus*, edited by Larry W. Hurtado and Paul L. Owen, 130–58. London: T&T Clark, 2011.

Hartman, Lars. *"Into the Name of the Lord Jesus": Baptism in the Early Church*. Edinburgh: T&T Clark, 1997.

Hay, David M. *Glory at the Right Hand: Psalm 110 in Early Christianity*. Nashville: Abingdon, 1973.

Hayman, Peter. "Monotheism: A Misused Word in Jewish Studies?" *Journal of Jewish Studies* 42 (1991): 1–15.

Hengel, Martin. "Abba, Maranatha, Hosanna und die Anfänge der Christologie." In *Studien zur Christologie, Kleine Schriften IV*, 496–534. Tübingen: Mohr Siebeck, 2006.

———. "Christology and New Testament Chronology." In *Between Jesus and Paul: Studies in the Earliest History of Christianity*, 30–47. London: SCM, 1983. First published in German 1972 by Theologischer Verlag (Zurich). "Christologie und neutestamentliche Chronologie: Zu einer Aporie in der Geschichte des Urchristentums." In *Neues Testament und Geschichte, Festschrift O. Cullmann*, edited by Heinrich Baltensweiler and Bo Reicke, 43–67.

———. "Hymns and Christology." In *Between Jesus and Paul: Studies in the Earliest History of Christianity*, 78–96. London: SCM, 1983.

———. *Judaism and Hellenism: Studies in the Encounter in Palestine During the Early Hellenistic Period*. 2 vols. London: SCM, 1974.

———. "'Sit at My Right Hand!' The Enthronement of Christ at the Right Hand of God and Psalm 110:1." In *Studies in Early Christology*, 119–225. Edinburgh: T&T Clark, 1995.

———. *Studies in Early Christology*. Edinburgh: T&T Clark, 1995.

———. *The "Hellenization" of Judaea in the First Century after Christ*. London: SCM, 1989.

———. *The Son of God: The Origin of Christology and the History of Jewish-Hellenistic Religion*. Philadelphia: Fortress Press, 1976.

Hopkins, Keith. *A World Full of Gods: Pagans, Jews, and Christians in the Roman Empire*. London: Weidenfeld & Nicolson, 1999.

Hurtado, Larry W. "'Ancient Jewish Monotheism' in the Hellenistic and Roman Periods." *Journal of Ancient Judaism* 4 (2013): 379–400.

———. *At the Origins of Christian Worship: The Context and Character of Earliest Christian Devotion*. Grand Rapids: Eerdmans, 1999.

— — —. "Christ-Devotion in the First Two Centuries: Reflections and a Proposal." *Toronto Journal of Theology* 12 (1996): 17–33.

— — —. *Destroyer of the Gods: Early Christian Distinctiveness in the Roman World*. Waco, TX: Baylor University Press, 2016.

— — —. "Early Christological Interpretation of the Messianic Psalms." *Salmanticensis* 64 (2017): 73–100. Reprinted in Larry W. Hurtado, *Ancient Jewish Monotheism and Early Christian Jesus-Devotion: The Context and Character of Christological Faith*, 559–82. Waco, TX: Baylor University Press, 2017.

— — —. "First Century Jewish Monotheism." *Journal for the Study of the New Testament* 71 (1998): 3–26. Reprinted in Larry W. Hurtado, *How on Earth Did Jesus Become a God? Historical Questions about Earliest Devotion to Jesus*, 111–33. Grand Rapids: Eerdmans, 2005.

— — —. *God in New Testament Theology*. Nashville: Abingdon, 2010.

— — —. *How on Earth Did Jesus Become a God? Historical Questions about Earliest Devotion to Jesus*. Grand Rapids: Eerdmans, 2005.

— — —. "Jesus' Divine Sonship in Paul's Epistle to the Romans." In *Romans and the People of God*, edited by Sven K. Soderlund and N. T. Wright, 217–33. Grand Rapids: Eerdmans, 1999.

— — —. *Lord Jesus Christ: Devotion to Jesus in Earliest Christianity*. Grand Rapids: Eerdmans, 2003.

— — —. "Monotheism, Principal Angels, and the Background of Christology." In *The Oxford Handbook of the Dead Sea Scrolls*, edited by Timothy H. Lim and John J. Collins, 546–64. Oxford: Oxford University Press, 2010.

— — —. "New Testament Christology: A Critique of Bousset's Influence." *Theological Studies* 40 (1979): 306–17.

— — —. *One God, One Lord: Early Christian Devotion and Ancient Jewish Monotheism*. Philadelphia: Fortress Press; London: SCM, 1988. 2nd ed., Edinburgh: T&T Clark, 1998. 3rd ed., London: Bloomsbury/T&T Clark, 2015.

— — —. "Pre-70 CE Jewish Opposition to Christ-Devotion." *Journal of Theological Studies* 50 (1999): 50–57. Reprinted in Hurtado, *How on Earth Did Jesus Become a God?*, 152–78. Grand Rapids: Eerdmans, 2005.

———. "Religious Experience and Religious Innovation in the New Testament." Journal of Religion 80 (2000): 183–205. Reprinted in Hurtado, How on Earth Did Jesus Become a God?, 179–204. Grand Rapids: Eerdmans, 2005.

———. "Remembering and Revelation: The Historic and Glorified Jesus in the Gospel of John." In Israel's God and Rebecca's Children: Christology and Community in Early Judaism and Christianity, edited by David B. Capes, et al., 195–213. Waco, TX: Baylor University Press, 2007.

———. "Revelatory Experiences and Religious Innovation in Earliest Christianity." Expository Times 125 (2014): 469–82.

———. Review of Angel Veneration and Christology by Loren T. Stuckenbruck. Journal of Theological Studies 47 (1996): 248–53.

———. Review of Did the First Christians Worship Jesus? by J. D. G. Dunn. Journal of Theological Studies 61 (2010): 736–40.

———. Review of Did the First Christians Worship Jesus? The New Testament Evidence by James D. G. Dunn. Larry Hurtado's Blog. https://larryhurtado.files.wordpress.com/2010/07/dunn-was-jesus-worshipped-review.pdf.

———. Review of The Only True God: Early Christian Monotheism in Its Jewish Context by James F. McGrath. Larry Hurtado's Blog. https://larryhurtado.files.wordpress.com/2010/07/mc-grath-reveiw-essay1.pdf.

———. "The Place of Jesus in Earliest Christian Prayer and Its Import for Early Christian Identity." In Early Christian Prayer and Identity Formation, edited by Reidar Hvalvik and Karl Olav Sandnes, 35–56. Tübingen: Mohr Siebeck, 2014. Reprinted in Hurtado, Ancient Jewish Monotheism and Jesus-Devotion: The Context and Character of Early Christological Faith, 625–34. Waco, TX: Baylor University Press, 2017.

———. "Son of God." In Dictionary of Paul and His Letters, edited by Gerald F. Hawthorne, Ralph P. Martin, and Daniel G. Reid, 900–6. Downers Grove, IL: InterVarsity Press, 1993.

———. "The 'Son of God' in/and the Roman Empire: A Review Essay." Larry Hurtado's Blog. https://larryhurtado.wordpress.com/

2013/01/17/the-son-of-god-inand-the-roman-empire-a-re-viewessay/.

———. "Wilhelm Bousset's Kyrios Christos: An Appreciative and Critical Assessment." *Early Christianity* 6 (2015): 1–13.

———. "Worship and Divine Identity: Richard Bauckham's Christological Pilgrimage." In *In the Fullness of Time: Essays on Christology, Creation, and Eschatology in Honor of Richard Bauckham*, edited by Daniel M. Gurner, Grant Macaskill, and Jonathan T. Pennington, 82–96. Grand Rapids: Eerdmans, 2016.

———. "YHWH's Return to Zion: A New Catalyst for Earliest High Christology?" In *God and the Faithfulness of Paul*, edited by Christoph Heilig, J. Thomas Hewitt, and Michael F. Bird, 417–38. Tübingen: Mohr Siebeck, 2016.

Johnson, Norman B. *Prayer in the Apocrypha and Pseudepigrapha: A Study of the Jewish Concept of God.* SBLMS 2. Philadelphia: Society of Biblical Literature, 1948.

Jonquiere, Tessel M. *Prayer in Josephus.* AJEC 70. Leiden: Brill, 2007.

Jungmann, Joseph. *The Place of Christ in Liturgical Prayer.* Translated by A. Peeler. 2nd ed. London: Geoffrey Chapman, 1965.

King, Charles. "The Organization of Roman Religious Beliefs." *Classical Antiquity* 22 (2003): 275–312.

Kirchschläger, W. "ἐπικαλέω." In Vol. 2 of *Exegetical Dictionary of the New Testament*, ed. Horst Balz and Gerhard Schneider, 28–29. Grand Rapids: Eerdmans, 1990–93.

Kodell, Jerome. *The Eucharist in the New Testament.* Wilmington, DE: Michael Glazier, 1988.

Kramer, Werner. *Christ, Lord, Son of God.* SBT 50. Naperville: Allenson, 1966.

Kreitzer, Larry J. *Jesus and God in Paul's Eschatology.* JSNTSup 19. Sheffield: JSOT Press, 1987.

Kroll, Joseph. *Die christliche Hymnodik bis zu Klemens von Alexandreia.* Königsberg: Hartungsche Buchdruckerei, 1921.

Kuhn, K. G. "The Lord's Supper and the Communal Meal at Qumran." In *The Scrolls and the New Testament*, edited by Krister Stendahl, 65–93. London: SCM, 1958. Reprint, New York: Crossroad, 1992.

Kümmel, Werner G. *The New Testament: The History of the Investigation of Its Problems*. Translated by S. McLean Gilmour and Howard C. Kee. Nashville: Abingdon, 1972.

Lattke, Michael. *Hymnus: Materialien zu einer Geschichte der antiken Hymnologie*. NTOA 19. Göttingen: Vandenhoeck & Ruprecht; Fribourg: Editions universitaires, 1991.

Leonhard, Clemens, and Hermut Löhr, eds. *Literature or Liturgy? Early Christian Hymns and Prayers in Their Literary and Liturgical Context in Antiquity*. Tübingen: Mohr Siebeck, 2014.

Machen, J. Gresham. *The Origin of Paul's Religion*. London: Hodder & Stoughton, 1921. Reprint, New York: Macmillan, 1925.

Mack, Burton. *A Myth of Innocence: Mark and Christian Origins*. Philadelphia: Fortress Press, 1988.

MacMullen, Ramsay. *Paganism in the Roman Empire*. New Haven: Yale University Press, 1981.

Marchal, Joseph A. "Expecting a Hymn, Encountering an Argument: Introducing the Rhetoric of Philippians and Pauline Interpretation." *Interpretation* 61 (2007): 245-55.

Martin, Michael Wade, and Bryan A. Nash. "Philippians 2:6-11 as Subversive Hymnos: A Study in the Light of Ancient Rhetorical Theory." *Journal of Theological Studies* 66 (2015): 90-138.

Martin, Ralph, and Brian Dodd, eds. *Where Christology Began: Essays on Philippians 2*. Louisville: Westminster John Knox, 1998.

Matlock, Michael. *Discovering the Traditions of Prose Prayers in Early Jewish Literature*. LSTS 81. London: T&T Clark, 2012.

McGiffert, Arthur Cushman. *The God of the Early Christians*. Edinburgh: T&T Clark, 1924.

McGrath, James F. *The Only True God: Early Christian Monotheism in Its Jewish Context*. Urbana, IL: University of Illinois Press, 2009.

Milik, J. T., ed. *The Books of Enoch: Aramaic Fragments of Qumran Cave 4*. Oxford: Clarendon, 1976.

Millar, Fergus. *The Emperor in the Roman World, 31 B.C.-A.D. 337*. Ithaca, NY: Cornell University Press, 1977.

Newman, Carey C. *Paul's Glory-Christology: Tradition and Rhetoric*. NovTSup 69. Leiden: Brill, 1992.

Nickelsburg, George W. E., and James C. VanderKam. 1 *Enoch: The Hermeneia Translation*. Minneapolis: Fortress, 2012.

Nilsson, M. P. "Pagan Divine Service in Late Antiquity." *Harvard Theological Review* 38 (1945): 63–69.

Nongbri, Brent. *Before Religion: A History of a Modern Concept*. New Haven: Yale University Press, 2013.

Novenson, Matthew V. *Christ among the Messiahs: Christ Language in Paul and Messiah Language in Ancient Judaism*. New York: Oxford University Press, 2012.

O'Brien, Peter T. "Benediction, Blessing, Doxology, Thanksgiving." In *Dictionary of Paul and His Letters*, edited by Gerald F. Hawthorne, Ralph P. Martin, and Daniel G. Reid, 68–71. Downers Grove, IL: InterVarsity Press, 1993.

Paschke, Boris A. "Tertullian on Liturgical Prayer to Christ: New Insights from De Spect. 25.5 and Apol. 2.6." *Vigiliae Christianae* 65 (2011): 1–10.

Peppard, Michael. "'Poetry,' 'Hymns' and 'Traditional Material' in New Testament Epistles or How to Do Things with Indentations." *Journal for the Study of the New Testament* 30 (2008): 319–42.

———. *The Son of God in the Roman World: Divine Sonship in Its Social and Political Context*. New York: Oxford University Press, 2011.

Perrin, Norman. "Reflections on the Publication in English of Bousset's Kyrios Christos." *Expository Times* 82 (1971): 340–42.

Pinsent, John. "Roman Spirituality." In *Classical Mediterranean Spirituality*, edited by A. H. Armstrong, 154–94. New York: Crossroad, 1986.

Price, Simon R. F. *Rituals and Power: The Roman Imperial Cult in Asia Minor*. Cambridge, UK: Cambridge University Press, 1984.

Rawlinson, A. E. J. *The New Testament Doctrine of Christ*. London: Longmans, Green, 1926.

Schäfer, Peter. "Magic and Religion in Ancient Judaism." In *Envisioning Magic: A Princeton Seminar and Symposium*, edited by Peter Schäfer and Hans G. Kippenberg, 19–44. Leiden: Brill, 1997.

Sherwin-White, A. N. *The Letters of Pliny: A Historical and Social Commentary*. Oxford: Clarendon, 1966.

Smith, Dennis E. *From Symposium to Eucharist: The Banquet in the Early Christian World*. Minneapolis: Fortress, 2003.

Smith, Mark S. *The Early History of God*. San Francisco: Harper & Row, 1990.

Stendahl, Krister. "Paul and the Introspective Conscience of the West." *Harvard Theological Review* 56 (1963): 199–215. Reprinted in Stendahl, *Paul among Jews and Gentiles*, 78–96. Philadelphia: Fortress Press, 1976.

Stevenson, J., ed. *A New Eusebius*. London: SPCK, 1974.

Strawbridge, Jennifer R., and Benjamin Edsall. "The Songs We Used to Sing? Hymn 'Traditions' and Reception in Pauline Letters." *Journal for the Study of the New Testament* 37 (2015): 290–311.

Stuckenbruck, Loren T. *Angel Veneration and Christology*. WUNT 2/70. Tübingen: J. C. B. Mohr [Siebeck], 1995.

Teixidor, Javier. *The Pagan God: Popular Religion in the Graeco-Roman Near East*. Princeton: Princeton University Press, 1977.

Thiselton, Anthony C. *The First Epistle to the Corinthians: A Commentary on the Greek Text*. NIGTC. Grand Rapids: Eerdmans, 2000.

Thompson, Leonard L. "Hymns in Early Christian Worship." *Anglican Theological Review* 55 (1973): 458–72.

Vos, Geerhardus. "The Kyrios Christos Controversy." *Princeton Theological Review* 15 (1917): 21–89.

Waddell, James A. *The Messiah: A Comparative Study of the Enochic Son of Man and the Pauline Kyrios*. London: T&T Clark, 2011.

Weinfeld, Moshe. "Prayer and Liturgical Practice in the Qumran Sect." In *The Dead Sea Scrolls: Forty Years of Research*, edited by Devorah Dimant and Uriel Rappaport, 241–57. Leiden: Brill, 1992.

Weiss, Johannes. *The History of Primitive Christianity*. 2 vols. London: Macmillan, 1937. Reprinted as *Earliest Christianity*. New York: Harper & Brothers, 1959. First published in German as *Das Urchristentum*, 1917 by Vandenhoeck & Ruprecht (Göttingen).

Wernle, Paul. "Jesus und Paulus: Antitheses zu Bousset's Kyrios Christos." *Zeitschrift für Theologie und Kirche* 25 (1915): 1–92.

Wilcox, Max. "'Upon the Tree'—Deut 21:22-23 in the New Testament." *Journal of Biblical Literature* 96 (1977): 85–99.

Wilken, Robert L. *The Christians as the Romans Saw Them*. New Haven: Yale University Press, 1984.

Yarbro Collins, Adela. "'How on Earth Did Jesus Become a God?' A Reply." In *Israel's God and Rebecca's Children: Christology and Community in Early Judaism and Christianity*, edited by David B. Capes, et al., 55–66. Waco, TX: Baylor University Press, 2007.

———. "The Worship of Jesus and the Imperial Cult." In *The Jewish Roots of Christological Monotheism: Papers From the St. Andrews Conference on the Historical Origins of the Worship of Jesus*, edited by Carey C. Newman, James R. Davila, and Gladys S. Lewis, 234–57. Leiden: Brill, 1999.

Yerkes, Royden Keith. *Sacrifice in Greek and Roman Religions and Early Judaism*. London: Black, 1953.

SUBJECT AND AUTHOR INDEX

SCRIPTURE INDEX

Old Testament

New Testament

Apocrypha

Pseudepigrapha

Other Ancient Sources

Josephus

Jewish War

Philo of Alexandria

Decal.

Pliny

Epistles